January 17, 2012

The Secrets of the Psalms

*Miraculous Meanings
in the Bible's Most Inspiring Book*

Amazon.com

The Secrets of the Psalms

Miraculous Meanings
in the Bible's Most Inspiring Book

REVEREND
CHESTINA MITCHELL ARCHIBALD

Produced by The Philip Lief Group, Inc.

BERKLEY BOOKS, NEW YORK

The Biblical quotations used in this volume are
from the King James Version.

This book is an original publication of The Berkley Publishing Group.

THE SECRETS OF THE PSALMS

A Berkley Book / published by arrangement with
The Philip Lief Group

PRINTING HISTORY
Berkley trade paperback edition / September 1999

The Penguin Putnam Inc. World Wide Web site address is
http://www.penguinputnam.com

ISBN: 0-425-17043-8

BERKLEY®
Berkley Books are published by The Berkley Publishing Group,
a division of Penguin Putnam Inc.,
375 Hudson Street, New York, New York 10014.
BERKLEY and the "B" design
are trademarks belonging to Penguin Putnam Inc.

PRINTED IN THE UNITED STATES OF AMERICA

10 9 8 7 6 5 4 3 2 1

This work is dedicated to the loving memory of my sister, Lenora Mitchell Johnson, and my brother, David Mitchell, who have both transcended this sphere, yet remain my angels at unawares; to both Reverend Shirley Majors-Jones and Reverend George P. Lee, who made me stay focused until this project was completed; to Reverend Henry R. Delaney, who contributed much to the compilation of Scriptural references, to my son Albert J. Archibald, III, who is a constant source of joy and inspiration, and to all my children and friends, who are now and shall become as we walk this path together.

Contents

Psalms for Protection When Taking a Journey

Psalms for Healing

Psalms for Gaining Wealth

Psalms for Help in Stressful Situations

Psalms for Overcoming Enemies

Psalms for Finding True Love

Psalms for Gaining Confidence

Psalms for Coping with Emotions

Psalms for Relief from Suffering

Psalms for Blessings on Important Occasions

Psalms for Happiness

Psalms of Affirmation

Psalms for Finding Guidance

Psalms for Aid in Spiritual Quest

Psalms of Praise and Thanksgiving

The Book of Psalms (King James Version)

Introduction

In the fourth century, Augustine of Hippo, North Africa, said, "Thou hast made us for thyself, O Lord, and our hearts are restless until they find rest in thee." Here at the end of the twentieth century, when life can seem overwhelming, persons from every walk of life hunger for rest in the Lord. They seek nurture for their parched souls. They search for ways to affirm their spirituality and enter the enlightened path of spiritual growth. They long to enhance their personal power and experience true joy. All know that there is more to life than what the eye can perceive. Many realize there are ways to create links with forces in the spiritual world to make life better. But few know how to tap into these eternal powers.

For centuries spiritual seekers have believed that the psalms hold a key to true power. Those who have diligently deciphered their meanings have reaped the benefits of that power. "A man's belly shall be satisfied with the fruit of his mouth; and with the increase of his lips shall he be filled. Death and life are in the power of the tongue: and they that love it shall eat the fruit thereof" (Proverbs, 18: 20–21). Certainly the 150 psalms in the Old Testament lead us to the core of the mystery that is God. *The Secrets of the Psalms* will help you not only understand the heart of God better, but it will also help you tap the mystical power in the Word of God.

The Secrets of the Psalms is designed for all who seek to grow spiritually. Saint Paul wrote to the Corinthians that the person who lives without the Spirit "receiveth not the things of the Spirit of God . . . neither can he know them, because they are spiritually discerned" (I Corinthians 2:14). This book will help you meditate on how the psalms can be used to discern the spiritual element in the rhythms of your everyday life. To learn the secrets of the psalms, you need only to approach them with a simple inward piety. If you stand humbly in the presence of God while speaking the psalms, their power will wash over you, and you will find that you have eyes to see and ears to hear. When you experience the messages of the psalms in your everyday life, your hope is raised and your life takes on new meaning. You awake to the ways God intervenes in your life.

The most profound human desires are for inner peace, success, and freedom. By compiling *The Secrets of the Psalms*, I want to help seekers receive their hearts' desire and live more effective and satisfying lives. It is my hope that the spiritual discoveries you will make in reading this book will enable you to live anew by exploring the miraculous meanings embedded in this ancient book.

—Reverend Chestina Mitchell Archibald
Nashville, Tennessee

Psalms for Blessings

For Blessing Newlyweds

*M*arriage is an honorable estate instituted by God. You should not enter into it unadvisedly, but reverently, discreetly, and in the fear of God. If you love one another and let God's love be perfected in both of you, your union will not only be pleasing to God, but will also serve as a sanctuary for you and your family. If you are contemplating marriage, read verses 6–9 of Psalm 28. God will graciously bless you and yours.

PSALM 28
Verses 6–9

⁶ Blessed be the Lord, because he hath heard the voice of my supplications.

⁷ The Lord is my strength and my shield; my heart trusted in him, and I am helped: therefore my heart greatly rejoiceth; and with my song will I praise him.

⁸ The Lord is their strength, and he is the saving strength of his anointed.

⁹ Save thy people, and bless thine inheritance: feed them also, and lift them up for ever.

FOR BLESSING PARENTS

*W*hen you become a parent you become a cocreator with God. If you walk with integrity, your children will be blessed with your name and your name shall be remembered throughout many generations. When you teach your children to exalt God, you are doubly blessed. Parents can be blessed by reading verses 16 and 17 of Psalm 45.

PSALM 45
Verses 16–17

[16] Instead of thy fathers shall be thy children, whom thou mayest make princes in all the earth.

[17] I will make thy name to be remembered in all generations: therefore shall the people praise thee for ever and ever.

FOR BLESSING A NEWBORN

$\mathcal{T}$he gift of life comes only by the omnipotence of God. A newborn child manifests the glory, majesty, and providence of God. Many psalms describe a creator who is a faithful God, but verse 3 of Psalm 127 and verse 9 of Psalm 113, read constantly, are sure to bless a newborn.

PSALM 127
Verse 3

³ Lo, children are an heritage of the Lord: and the fruit of the womb is his reward.

PSALM 113
Verse 9

⁹ He maketh the barren woman to keep house, and to be a joyful mother of children. Praise ye the Lord.

FOR BLESSING A CHILD

A child should be taught early to seek the Lord, and the child will grow in wisdom as he grows in age. The child will one day be able to say: "When I was a child, I spoke like a child; I thought like a child; I reasoned like a child; When I became an adult, I put an end to childish ways." (I Corinthians 13:11). Always commit your child to God's care. Discipline your child. Live an exemplary life before your child. Ask God for a spirit of love and compassion. Then read verse 11 of Psalm 34 and verse 10 of Psalm 27.

PSALM 34
Verse 11

[11] Come, ye children, hearken unto me: I will teach you the fear of the Lord.

PSALM 27
Verse 10

[10] When my father and my mother forsake me, then the Lord will take me up.

FOR BLESSING FAMILY MEMBERS

$\mathcal{G}$od has given you a heart to know him. You will never be satisfied or able to experience true joy until you have an intimate relationship with God. God has a purpose for your life, and God has placed you among people who can help you bring that purpose to fruition. Family members have a special connectedness—they are gifts to one another. But sometimes family members forget to fulfill God's plan. To remain steadfast in your responsibility toward your family, and to help others remain steadfast as well, read Psalm 68:5 and 9; Psalm 32:1–2; and Psalm 146:1, 3, and 5.

PSALM 68
Verses 5, 9

⁵ A father of the fatherless, and a judge of the widows, is God in his holy habitation.

⁹ Thou, O God, didst send a plentiful rain, whereby thou didst confirm thine inheritance, when it was weary.

PSALM 32
Verses 1–2

¹ Blessed is he whose transgression is forgiven, whose sin is covered.

² Blessed is the man unto whom the Lord imputeth not iniquity, and in whose spirit there is no guile.

PSALM 146
Verses 1,3,5

[1] Praise ye the Lord. Praise the Lord, O my soul.

[3] Put not your trust in princes, nor in the son of man, in whom there is no help.

[5] Happy is he that hath the God of Jacob for his help, whose hope is in the Lord his God:

FOR BLESSING FRIENDS

*J*esus said that there is no greater love than the love of one who will lay down his life for a friend. If you are a true friend, surely you are concerned about the welfare of your friends and wish blessings for them as well as for yourself. As friends interact they help each other climb spiritual ladders—to be kind, loving, wise, compassionate, and knowing. True friends are rare and should be cherished as precious jewels. When desiring blessings for friends read verses 97:1, 11–12.

PSALM 97
Verses 1, 11–12

¹ The Lord reigneth; let the earth rejoice; let the multitude of isles be glad thereof.

¹¹ Light is sown for the righteous, and gladness for the upright in heart.

¹² Rejoice in the Lord, ye righteous; and give thanks at the remembrance of his holiness.

FOR BLESSING ONE'S BUSINESS COLLEAGUES

Colleagues in business are similar to friends. However, the relationship often goes through more strenuous tests. If your partner deals with a slack hand, it may affect your livelihood and your reputation. A colleague's diligence increases your profits. Because of this close association, it is a good thing to desire blessings for your business colleagues. Read Psalm 107: 23–24 to obtain your desired result.

PSALM 107
Verses 23–24

23 They that go down to the sea in ships, that do business in great waters;

24 These see the works of the Lord, and his wonders in the deep.

FOR BLESSING ONE'S WORK

*I*f you are faithful over little jobs, God will elevate you to greater responsibilities. The Lord will reward you for what you have done. The Lord will bless. Continue to serve the Lord with gladness. Seek to do the will of Jehovah. Be obedient to God's instructions. God desires you to serve him. If you do this, you shall see your work finished, and your family shall eat and rejoice in the fruits of your labor. Read Psalm 8: 3–7, and you will labor not in vain.

PSALM 8
Verses 3–7

³ When I consider thy heavens, the work of thy fingers, the moon and the stars, which thou hast ordained;

⁴ What is man, that thou art mindful of him? and the son of man, that thou visitest him?

⁵ For thou hast made him a little lower than the angels, and hast crowned him with glory and honour.

⁶ Thou madest him to have dominion over the works of thy hands; thou hast put all things under his feet;

⁷ All sheep and oxen, yea, and the beasts of the field;

For Blessing One's Home

"*T*hrough wisdom is an house builded; and by understanding it is established; And by knowledge shall the chambers be filled with all precious and pleasant riches" (Proverbs 24:3–4). Your home is blessed when God is the head of it. When God's presence is acknowledged in a house, inhabitants of that house love each other as God has commanded, and that house becomes a home. Proverbs lists three properties that make a house a home: knowledge, understanding, and wisdom. Read constantly verse 1 of Psalm 127 and have a blessed home.

PSALM 127
Verse 1

[1] Except the Lord build the house, they labour in
vain that build it: except the Lord keep the city,
the watchman waketh but in vain.

FOR BLESSING ONE'S CHURCH

*T*he church is God's house. It is a place set aside for persons to worship God, our creator. It is a place to give thanks to God in great congregations and to praise God even as "two or three gather together." (Matthew 18:20) But a church *building* cannot embrace the fullness of God for heaven is God's throne and earth is God's footstool. No house can be built for Him. The real church, then, is the fellowship of people. God's desire is that people will come together on God's Holy Hill that he might make them joyous. To bless your church read Psalm 35:18, Psalm 122:1–2, 6, and 9, and Psalm 24:3–7.

PSALM 35
Verse 18

[18] I will give thee thanks in the great congregation: I will praise thee among much people.

PSALM 122
Verses 1–2, 6, 9

[1] I was glad when thy said unto me, Let us go into the house of the Lord.

[2] Our feet shall stand within thy gates, O Jerusalem.

[6] Pray for the peace of Jerusalem: they shall prosper that love thee.

[9] Because of the house of the Lord our God I will seek thy good.

PSALM 24
Verses 3–7

[3] Who shall ascend into the hill of the Lord? or who shall stand in his holy place?

⁴ He that hath clean hands, and a pure heart; who hath not lifted up his soul unto vanity, nor sworn deceitfully.

⁵ He shall receive the blessing from the Lord, and righteousness from the God of his salvation.

⁶ This is the generation of them that seek him, that seek thy face, O Jacob. Selah.

⁷ Lift up your heads, O ye gates; and be ye lift up, ye everlasting doors; and the King of glory shall come in.

FOR AN ABUNDANT HARVEST

*T*o have an abundant harvest, seek the Lord and sow seeds in abundance. Eventually you will reap the fruits of your labor. Malachi 3:10 states, "Bring ye all the tithes into the storehouse, . . . I will pour you out a blessing, that there shall not be room enough to receive it." No good thing will God withhold for them that diligently seek him. Great is God's goodness, which thou hast laid up for them that fear God. To reap an abundant harvest in every way, read Psalm 65:4, 9–12.

PSALM 65
Verses 4, 9–12

⁴ Blessed is the man whom thou choosest, and causest to approach unto thee, that he may dwell in thy courts: we shall be satisfied with the goodness of thy house, even of thy holy temple.

⁹ Thou visitest the earth, and waterest it: thou greatly enrichest it with the river of God, which is full of water: thou preparest them corn, when thou hast so provided for it.

¹⁰ Thou waterest the ridges thereof abundantly: thou settlest the furrows thereof: thou makest it soft with showers: thou blessest the springing thereof.

¹¹ Thou crownest the year with thy goodness: and the little hills rejoice on every side.

¹² They drop upon the pastures of the wilderness: and the little hills rejoice on every side.

Psalms for Protection

FROM ILLNESS

Verse 2 of Psalm 30 and verse 17 of Psalm 118 are potent scriptures to read when faced with illness. To affirm the end result of our asking in faith is the first step toward being healed. It also exalts God. Throughout scripture, God promises to heal and protect from illness all those who diligently harken unto the voice of the Lord.

PSALM 30
Verse 2

[2] O Lord my God, I cried unto thee, and thou hast healed me.

PSALM 118
Verse 17

[17] I shall not die, but live, and declare the works of the Lord.

FROM FEAR

Anxiety and fear caused by the perception of impending danger or misfortune can paralyze you and prevent you from taking right action. Relief comes by concentrating on verses 1–2 of Psalm 37. If the fear is associated with an adversary, it is good to read the entire psalm. It is also important to note that fear itself is dangerous. It draws to you that which you fear.

PSALM 37
Verses 1–2

¹ Fret not thyself because of evildoers, neither be thou envious against the workers of iniquity.

² For they shall soon be cut down like the grass, and wither as the green herb.

FROM VIOLENCE

*I*n the face of a harsh, rough, destructive force—be it either physical force or intense emotional force—only God can deliver you. Verse 1 of Psalm 70 and verse 10 of Psalm 58 should perhaps be committed to memory and recited constantly when it appears that wickedness may erupt into violence.

PSALM 70
Verse 1

¹ Make haste, O God to deliver me; make haste to help me, O Lord.

PSALM 58
Verse 10

¹⁰ The righteous shall rejoice when he seeth the vengeance: he shall wash his feet in the blood of the wicked.

FROM HOSTILE ATTITUDES

*H*ostile attitudes usually lead to evil thoughts. Once adversaries begin to think evil, they soon began to speak evil and eventually they will act in evil ways. They may even gather others to oppose you and be antagonistic toward you. But if you live a righteous life and cry unto the Lord, the hand of God will deliver you. Read verses 34, 39, 40, and 37 in this order of Psalm 37.

PSALM 37
Verses 34, 39, 40, 37

³⁴ Wait on the Lord, and keep his way, and he shall exalt thee to inherit the land: when the wicked are cut off, thou shalt see it.

³⁹ But the salvation of the righteous is of the Lord: he is their strength in the time of trouble.

⁴⁰ And the Lord shall help them, and deliver them: he shall deliver them from the wicked, and save them, because they trust in him.

³⁷ Mark the perfect man, and behold the upright: for the end of that man is peace.

FROM EVIL INFLUENCES

*M*any injuries, and misfortunes can result from evil influences. To receive counsel is wise, but you must examine the source of the counsel you receive. Take care not to heed the advice of evil persons, nor desire to be in their company. Poor counsel always stops your progress. You can be running along in life at full speed, but when you get counsel from the ungodly, you start walking. The first of all the psalms admonishes you to discern between those who will lead you in the right path and those who will lead you in the wrong path. Read Psalm 1:1.

PSALM 1
Verse 1

[1] Blessed is the man that walketh not in the counsel of the ungodly, nor standeth in the way of sinners, nor sitteth in the seat of the scornful.

FROM EVIL THOUGHTS

*E*vil thoughts cause a person to have a downcast and disquieted soul. The antidote to evil thoughts is gratitude, because a grateful soul is a happy soul. No one can remember the wondrous deeds of the Lord and continue to hold evil thoughts. Verses 1, 2, and 5 of Psalm 105 help create a frame of mind that dissipates evil thoughts.

PSALM 105
Verses 1, 2, 5

¹ O give thanks unto the Lord; call upon his name: make known his deeds among the people.

² Sing unto him, sing psalms unto him: talk ye of all his wondrous works.

⁵ Remember his marvellous works that he hath done; his wonders, and the judgments of his mouth.

FROM PERSONAL WEAKNESS

*A*t some point in life you will yield to the temptations of an unsettled world. Disciplines that you thought you had mastered seem lost. You find yourself engaged in foolishness. When it happens, you will soon recognize in yourself a yearning to repent. At these times meditate on the words found in verses 1, 2, and 9 of Psalm 51.

PSALM 51
Verses 1, 2, 9

[1] Have mercy upon me, O God, according to thy lovingkindness: according unto the multitude of thy tender mercies blot out my transgressions.

[2] Wash me throughly from mine iniquity, and cleanse me from my sin.

[9] Hide thy face from my sins, and blot out all mine iniquities.

Psalms for Protection When Taking a Journey

➢

FOR SELF

When taking a journey, it is always advisable to intentionally seek God's protection. Many of us begin our journeys without consciously acknowledging God's abiding presence. God always stands ready to protect and assist us. All God requests is that we remain awake to his guardianship. When you are getting ready to undertake a journey, take time from your busy preparations to read and contemplate verses 6 and 7 of Psalm 28. In God's hand is power and might to protect you from all hurt and harm or danger.

PSALM 28
Verses 6, 7

⁶ Blessed be the Lord, because he hath heard the voice of my supplications.

⁷ The Lord is my strength and my shield; my heart trusted in him, and I am helped: therefore my heart greatly rejoiceth; and with my song will I praise him.

FOR SOMEONE ELSE

*W*hen we care about others, we want them to be safe. Whether loved ones are leaving home to establish independent living or just going on a short trip, our concern is the same. We want God to go with them. We want their journey to be pleasurable and beneficial, but we know that difficult situations sometimes arise for travelers. To dispel worry and send your loved ones on their way assured of God's protection, read Psalm 78:52–53, and 72.

PSALM 78
Verses 52–53, 72

⁵² But [God] made his own people to go forth like sheep, and guided them in the wilderness like a flock.

⁵³ And he led them on safely, so that they feared not: but the sea overwhelmed their enemies.

⁷² So he fed them according to the integrity of his heart; and guided them by the skilfulness of his hands.

FOR A CHILD LEAVING HOME

Scripture says if you bring up your children in the way they should go, when they are old they will not depart from it. All parents hope that their children will remember their teachings. Yet when a child is leaving home, anxiety comes calling. Parents must remember that children come from God. When a child leaves home it is time to let God complete the work that God began. Rest in the assurance that there are no limitations on God. God is everywhere that a parent cannot go. Read verses 5–6 of Psalm 36 and take solace in the Lord.

PSALM 36
Verses 5–6

⁵ Thy mercy, O Lord, is in the heavens; and thy faithfulness reacheth unto the clouds.

⁶ Thy righteousness is like the great mountains; thy judgments are a great deep: O Lord, thou preservest man and beast.

FOR MILITARY PERSONNEL

*W*ars and rumors of wars have plagued humans since the beginning of time. We know that if war breaks out, young men and women in the military will face a kind of danger they do not usually have to face. Some of us will lose loved ones. Therefore, when those close to us join the military ranks, we more eagerly seek God's protection, devoutly praying verses 1–2 of Psalm 91.

PSALM 91
Verses 1–2

¹ He that dwelleth in the secret place of the most High shall abide under the shadow of the Almighty.

² I will say of the Lord, He is my refuge and my fortress: my God; in him will I trust.

FOR SAYING GOODBYE

*O*urs is a transient society. It seems we are always seeing people off as they pass into and then out of our lives. Or we are saying goodbye, ourselves, as we leave the lives of others, having spent a short or long time with them. Sometimes the leave-taking is a happy occasion; sometimes it is bitter to say goodbye. Notwithstanding the circumstances that make it necessary to say goodbye, every traveler needs God's protection. How can you join God in blessing the traveler who leaves you—or those whom you leave behind? As you part, read Psalm 121.

PSALM 121
Verses 1–8

[1] I will lift up mine eyes unto the hills, from whence cometh my help?

[2] My help cometh from the Lord, which made heaven and earth.

[3] He will not suffer thy foot to be moved; he that keepeth thee will not slumber.

[4] Behold, he that keepeth Israel shall neither slumber nor sleep.

[5] The Lord is thy keeper: the Lord is thy shade upon thy right hand.

[6] The sun shall not smite thee by day, nor the moon by night.

[7] The Lord shall preserve thee from all evil: he shall preserve thy soul.

[8] The Lord shall preserve thy going out and thy coming in from this time forth, and even for evermore.

FOR LETTING GO

When someone or something has been a part of your life and then is no longer there, it may be difficult for you to let go. Change is always stressful. You may begin to doubt your identity or your ability to go on without that person or thing. In order to find peace within and protection for yourself when letting go, meditate on Psalm 46:1–3.

PSALM 46
Verses 1–3

¹ God is our refuge and strength, a very present help in trouble.

² Therefore will not we fear, though the earth be removed, and though the mountains be carried into the midst of the sea;

³ Though the waters thereof roar and be troubled, though the mountains shake with the swelling thereof. Selah.

Psalms for Healing

❧

FOR SELF

*T*he essence of human existence is perpetually to strive to become whole. Humans yearn to be whole in mind, body, and spirit. God, our creator, is the only one who can infuse our existence with this kind of balance. Healing practitioners now know that all facets of our bodies, minds, and spirits are interrelated. In seeking healing for yourself, you begin by acknowledging that you are walking in the light of God. This necessitates clearing your mind of all negativity and your life of anything that is not pure. When you walk in faith, healing of the mind and body is sure to come. To understand this principle and to remind yourself of it in times of need, read Psalm 21:1–4.

PSALM 21
Verses 1–4

¹ The king shall joy in thy strength, O Lord; and in thy salvation how greatly shall he rejoice!

² Thou hast given him his heart's desire, and hast not withholden the request of his lips. Selah.

³ For thou preventest him with the blessings of goodness: thou settest a crown of pure gold on his head.

⁴ He asked life of thee, and thou gavest it him, even length of days for ever and ever.

FOR SOMEONE ELSE

*I*t is difficult to see another suffer. This is true no matter what the cause. We desire mental, physical, and spiritual healing for those we care about. We try to *do* something. We offer advice. We turn to doctors. But often our loved ones fail to adhere to our counsel. Sometimes physicians seem not to know what to do.

Just to *desire* good for another is a form of intercessory prayer. Through prayer the struggling individual can openly receive whatever is necessary to bring forth healing. When desiring healing for another, include in your prayers thoughts from Psalm 61:1–2, and 6–7.

PSALM 61
Verses 1–2, 6–7

¹ Hear my cry, O God; attend unto my prayer.

² From the end of the earth will I cry unto thee, when my heart is overwhelmed: lead me to the rock that is higher than I.

⁶ Thou wilt prolong the king's life: and his years as many generations.

⁷ He shall abide before God for ever: O prepare mercy and truth, which may preserve him.

FOR ACUTE CONDITIONS

*W*hen a condition is critical, there is one doctor who has never lost a patient and one lawyer who has never lost a case, there is one who knows your beginning and your end. There is one who is so high, none can go over; so low, none can go under; so wide, none can go around. For this one, there is no condition so severe that it cannot be healed. When you rest in this assurance you learn to praise God even before there are visible results of your asking. Posture yourself before God and read verses 1 and 2 of Psalms 146, 147, 148, 149, and 150. Praise God.

PSALM 146
Verses 1–2

¹ Praise ye the Lord. Praise the Lord, O my soul.

² While I live will I praise the Lord: I will sing praises unto my God while I have any being.

PSALM 147
Verses 1–2

¹ Praise ye the Lord: for it is good to sing praises unto our God; for it is pleasant; and praise is comely.

² The Lord doth build up Jerusalem: he gathereth together the outcasts of Israel.

PSALM 148
Verses 1–2

¹ Praise ye the Lord. Praise ye the Lord from the heavens: praise him in the heights.

² Praise ye him, all his angels: praise ye him, all his hosts.

PSALM 149
Verses 1–2

[1] Praise ye the Lord. Sing unto the Lord a new song, and his praise in the congregation of saints.

[2] Let Israel rejoice in him that made him: let the children of Zion be joyful in their King,

PSALM 150
Verses 1–2

[1] Praise ye the Lord. Praise God in his sanctuary: praise him in the firmament of his power.

[2] Praise him for his mighty acts: praise him according to his excellent greatness.

FOR CHRONIC ILLNESS

*W*hen you have suffered severely for a long time, or watched a loved one suffer, you may come to question God or even to question whether or not God really exists. To trust God even in the worst of times is truly the test of your faith. Many have learned to draw nearer to God through trying times. When learning to trust God, you will also find the courage to wait on the Lord. "And we know that all things work together for good to them that love God, to them who are the called according to his purpose"(Romans 8:28). If you are chronically ill, don't give up, continue to read, and believe Psalm 30:1–3.

PSALM 30
Verses 1–3

[1] I will extol thee, O Lord; for thou hast lifted me up, and hast not made my foes to rejoice over me.

[2] O Lord my God, I cried unto thee, and thou hast healed me.

[3] O Lord, thou hast brought up my soul from the grave: thou hast kept me alive, that I should not go down to the pit.

For Safe Delivery of a Child

Sometimes we take the safe delivery of a child for granted today. However, there are still many times that the bringing forth of life has complications that endanger mother or child or both. We cannot take such a life-changing event for granted. Only God can create life. Therefore, for the safe delivery of a child, contemplate Psalm 66: 8–9.

PSALM 66
Verses 8–9

[8] O bless our God, ye people, and make the voice of his praise to be heard:

[9] Which holdeth our soul in life, and suffereth not our feet to be moved.

FOR PHYSICAL HEALING

*T*he human body is the Holy temple of the spirit of the Lord. When this temple is in disarray, the spirit is sometimes vexed. Yet, even when our spirit is exasperated, a conscious moment reminds us that with God all things are possible and nothing is possible without God. God is the vine and we are the branches. God wants us healed and we must break through with renewed strength of endurance until all distress leaves and God's ear inclines toward us. Read Psalm 102:3–5 and 12–13 as you make your petition before the Lord.

PSALM 102
Verses 3–5, 12–13

³ For my days are consumed like smoke, and my bones are burned as an hearth.

⁴ My heart is smitten, and withered like grass; so that I forget to eat my bread.

⁵ By reason of the voice of my groaning my bones cleave to my skin.

¹² But thou, O Lord, shalt endure for ever; and thy remembrance unto all generations.

¹³ Thou shalt arise, and have mercy upon Zion: for the time to favour her, yea, the set time, is come.

FOR EMOTIONAL HEALING

*I*nner healing is sometimes the most difficult task. The mind is delicate; yet it is also potent and powerful. It can cause us to live in joy or to languish in sorrow. It can fill with fear or shine with faith. It can embrace hate or love. Simple weariness can cause us to faint in our mind. We can forget who we are. In that forest of forgetfulness, it can seem impossible to call up the necessary strength to walk toward the light. If you are seeking emotional healing for yourself or a loved one, read verses 12, 11, and 1 of Psalm 31, in the order in which they are printed, and hold fast to the goodness of God.

PSALM 31
Verses 12, 11, 1

[12] I am forgotten as a dead man out of mind: I am like a broken vessel.

[11] I was a reproach among all mine enemies, but especially among my neighbours, and a fear to mine acquaintance: they that did see me without fled from me.

[1] In thee, O Lord, do I put my trust; let me never be ashamed: deliver me in thy righteousness.

FOR SPIRITUAL HEALING

*O*ften the key to physical and emotional healing lies in seeking first to heal the spirit. And in a sense, spiritual healing is the easiest of all. When we simply commit our spirit into the hands of the Lord, the heaviness that invades our spirits when we seek to have our own way disappears, and our broken spirits are mended. When we have received spiritual healing we are able to appreciate the gifts that God has placed in us—love, joy, and peace—and we use them with confidence. See Psalm 32:1–2.

PSALM 32
Verses 1–2

[1] Blessed is he whose transgression is forgiven, whose sin is covered.

[2] Blessed is the man unto whom the Lord imputeth not iniquity, and in whose spirit there is no guile.

Psalms for Gaining Wealth

WHEN BURDENED BY DEBT

Wealth is generally counted in material possessions. Yet we know that merely accumulating things never brings complete satisfaction. We know, in fact, that material possessions bring misery when accompanied by burdensome debt. Sometimes we go into debt by acquiring things that we cannot afford to impress folk that we don't even like. This is self-imposed oppression. Therefore, to rid yourself of debt, pray first for self-esteem and righteousness. Then read continually verses 21–23 of Psalm 37.

PSALM 37
Verses 21–23

21 The wicked borroweth, and payeth not again: but the righteous sheweth mercy, and giveth.

22 For such as be blessed of him shall inherit the earth; and they that be cursed of him shall be cut off.

23 The steps of a good man are ordered by the Lord: and he delighteth in his way.

WHEN DESIRING MORE

*C*onstant recitation of verses 5–6 of Psalm 23 and verse 24 of Psalm 104 evokes God's favor and enables you to affirm life and deny lack in any form. To "deny lack" and "affirm life" prepares you to become receptive to prosperity and abundance. The psalms secure in you an awareness of God as the ultimate source of all goodness.

PSALM 23
Verses 5–6

5 Thou preparest a table before me in the presence of mine enemies: thou anointest my head with oil; my cup runneth over.

6 Surely goodness and mercy shall follow me all the days of my life: and I will dwell in the house of the Lord for ever.

PSALM 104
Verse 24

24 O Lord, how manifold are thy works! in wisdom hast thou made them all: the earth is full of thy riches.

WHEN WANTING TO HELP OTHERS

God is generous and wants us to be the same. To find a way to help others is one of the surest ways for you to gain true wealth. The best way to help is not to give money—one donation vanishes quickly—but to help another develop a prosperous attitude. When you aspire to help others, share with them verses 1, 3, 15, and 18 of Psalm 72.

PSALM 72
Verses 1, 3, 15, 18

¹ Give the king thy judgments, O God, and thy righteousness unto the king's son.

³ The mountains shall bring peace to the people, and the little hills, by righteousness.

¹⁵ And he shall live, and to him shall be given of the gold of Sheba: prayer also shall be made for him continually; and daily shall he be praised.

¹⁸ Blessed be the Lord God, the God of Israel, who only doeth wondrous things.

WHEN PLANNING A PURCHASE

To purchase something that belongs to another can benefit both you and the seller. Never try to gain something for nothing. There is a reciprocal law of nature that says that what is put in to a project will determine what is received. You reap what you sow. Every action brings about a corresponding reaction. Thus, when planning a purchase keep the words of God's covenant and the Lord will make all you do prosper. Take heed to fulfill the statutes and judgment in all things, and covet nothing owned by others. Most important, do not deal treacherously. Remember the words of the psalmist in Psalm 122:6–7.

PSALM 122
Verses 6–7

⁶ Pray for the peace of Jerusalem: they shall prosper that love thee.

⁷ Peace be within thy walls, and prosperity within thy palaces.

WHEN BUYING A HOUSE

*V*erses 1–2 of Psalm 127 help you overcome the human frailties that can cause failure when you try to procure property. Many hurdles await you in the long process of being approved to buy a house—reviewing credit history, checking income, preparing financial statements, and more. When one acknowledges that God works in every aspect of human affairs, you can remain calm—making it easier to persevere in accomplishing these tasks and achieving the goal. When you have done all that can be done toward acquiring a home, you must trust God, go to sleep with a peaceful mind, and wake knowing the outcome will reflect God's will for you.

PSALM 127
Verses 1–2

¹ Except the Lord build the house, they labour in vain that build it: except the Lord keep the city, the watchman waketh but in vain.

² It is vain for you to rise up early, to sit up late, to eat the bread of sorrows: for so he giveth his beloved sleep.

WHEN STARTING A BUSINESS

*M*any divine truths have become clichés, and some people think that means they have lost their power. For example, a person entering into business might once have said, "God is my partner." It is not just a cliché. If you start a business with the knowledge that God is, indeed, your most trustworthy partner, your heart will greatly rejoice at the benefits gained therefrom. Though difficulties may arise, your business is sure to prosper. Read Psalm 8:5–7 and Psalm 9:1.

PSALM 8
Verses 5–7

⁵ For thou hast made him a little lower than the angels, and hast crowned him with glory and honour.

⁶ Thou madest him to have dominion over the works of thy hands; thou hast put all things under his feet;

⁷ All sheep and oxen, yea, and the beasts of the field;

PSALM 9
Verse 1

¹ I will praise thee, O Lord, with my whole heart: I will shew forth all thy marvellous works.

Psalms for Help in Stressful Situations

WHEN CONCERNED ABOUT FINANCES

*I*n a society that is heavily influenced by finances, if you have money you are preoccupied with trying to keep it; if you do not have money, you are preoccupied with trying to get it. Remember: "The Lord takes care of the birds of the air and wheat of the field." (Matthew 6:28) God will surely take care of you. Calmly "cast thy burden upon the Lord, and he shall sustain thee." (Psalm 55:22) Scripture offers a solution to worry about money that seems illogical to those who don't believe. Malachi 3:10 reminds us: "If you bring ye all the tithes into the storehouse . . . God will pour you out blessings that there shall not be room enough to receive." Begin to give one tenth of all your earnings and read verses 1–4 of Psalm 91 when you become overly concerned about your finances.

PSALM 91
Verses 1–4

¹ He that dwelleth in the secret place of the most High shall abide under the shadow of the Almighty.

² I will say of the Lord, He is my refuge and my fortress: my God; in him will I trust.

³ Surely he shall deliver thee from the snare of the fowler, and from the noisome pestilence.

⁴ He shall cover thee with his feathers, and under his wings shalt thou trust: his truth shall be thy shield and buckler.

WHEN STUDYING

*W*hen you undertake a course of study, you want to be successful. In order to do so, you must plan to become fully engaged in your pursuit. You must use your mind, body, and spirit. Above all, you must become teachable. Stress results when you try to chart your *own* course. Seek to be enlightened—to sit and learn at the feet of the master teacher. Psalm 119: 25–27 will help you in this undertaking.

PSALM 119
Verses 25–27

[25] My soul cleaveth unto the dust: quicken thou me according to thy word.

[26] I have declared thy ways, and thou heardest me: teach me thy statutes.

[27] Make me to understand the way of thy precepts: so shall I talk of thy wondrous works.

WHEN TAKING A CRUCIAL TEST

Sometimes we go overboard worrying about whether or not we will pass some crucial test. We exaggerate the importance of the outcome and make too much depend on it. This is a kind of oppression. Of course you will study and prepare to the maximum of your ability. God expects you to help yourself. But after you have done all you can, read verse 2 of Psalm 127.

PSALM 127
Verse 2

² It is vain for you to rise up early, to sit up late, to eat the bread of sorrows: for so he giveth his beloved sleep.

WHEN SEEKING EMPLOYMENT

Unemployment can cause much stress and anxiety. But to succeed in a search for a new job, you need a positive self-image and a belief in your ultimate success. Let the tension that comes from unemployment run its course. Then prepare yourself for the long process before you. Self-affirmation is essential in securing work. When seeking labor, read Psalm 34:7–10.

PSALM 34
Verses 7–10

[7] The angel of the Lord encampeth round about them that fear him, and delivereth them.

[8] O taste and see that the Lord is good: blessed is the man that trusteth in him.

[9] O fear the Lord, ye his saints: for there is no want to them that fear him.

[10] The young lions do lack and suffer hunger: but they that seek the Lord shall not want any good thing.

WHEN INTERVIEWING FOR A JOB

*T*he interview is the most stressful part of acquiring a job or position. Every word you say is evaluated. Yet there is no reason to fret. Through the inspiration of the Almighty, you can answer the interviewer's questions in a way that will put you in the best light. Put yourself in God's hands and ask that God's will be done throughout the interview. Then peruse Psalm 39, verse 1, and Psalm 111:2–5.

PSALM 39
Verse 1

¹ I said, I will take heed to my ways, that I sin not with my tongue: I will keep my mouth with a bridle. . . .

PSALM 111
Verses 2–5

² The works of the Lord are great, sought out of all them that have pleasure therein.

³ His work is honourable and glorious: and his righteousness endureth for ever.

⁴ He hath made his wonderful works to be re-membered: the Lord is gracious and full of com-passion.

⁵ He hath given meat unto them that fear him: he will ever be mindful of his covenant.

WHEN ATTENDING AN IMPORTANT MEETING

*I*f you are worried about your performance at an important meeting, know that you are in God's favor and that God will guide the words of your mouth. God will enlighten you and give you spiritual vision that shines in the dark. Read verses 105 and 92, in that order, of Psalm 119 before the meeting starts and again when the meeting ends.

PSALM 119
Verses 105, 92

[105] Thy word is a lamp unto my feet, and a light unto my path.

[92] Unless thy law had been my delights, I should then have perished in mine affliction.

WHEN STARTING A JOB

*B*eginning a new job—learning new tasks and meeting new people—can cause anxiety. Begin by affirming that this job is a blessing from the Lord. Know that God is not as concerned with your *capability* as with your *availability*. If you allow God to work through you, and you do the job as if you are doing it for God, be assured that all will turn out well. As you enter into new employment, read daily Psalm 40: 1, 3–5.

PSALM 40
Verses 1, 3–5

[1] I waited patiently for the Lord; and he inclined unto me, and heard my cry.

[3] And he hath put a new song in my mouth, even praise unto our God: many shall see it, and fear, and shall trust in the Lord.

[4] Blessed is that man that maketh the Lord his trust, and respecteth not the proud, nor such as turn aside to lies.

[5] Many, O Lord my God, are thy wonderful works which thou hast done, and thy thoughts which are for us: they cannot be reckoned up in order unto thee: if I would declare and speak of them, they are more than can be numbered.

WHEN REQUESTING A RAISE

*W*hen requesting a raise, there are several questions you should ask yourself: Have you come to work on time? Did you work hard and smart? In other words, did you accomplish the tasks that were set before you? One gets paid for the work that is performed and the benefits it yields to the employer. Therefore, did your work benefit the employer? Do you bring peace and joy to the workplace? Or do you create problems for your coworkers? If your work deserves more compensation, request your raise with conviction and poise. For courage, read Psalm 27, verse 1, and Psalm 31, verse 24.

PSALM 27
Verse 1

¹ The Lord is my light and my salvation; whom shall I fear? the Lord is the strength of my life; of whom shall I be afraid?

PSALM 31
Verse 24

²⁴ Be of good courage, and he shall strengthen your heart, all ye that hope in the Lord.

When Seeking Advancement

*E*veryone in the Divine Order desires to improve. Progress is godly. However, the search for secular advancement based upon the evaluation of other humans can be stressful. When what you desire is in keeping with what God wills for you, there is peace not stress. When you seek God first, elevation takes on a different meaning and all things are soon added unto you. Read Psalm 21:1–5.

PSALM 21
Verses 1–5

¹ The king shall joy in thy strength, O Lord; and in thy salvation how greatly shall he rejoice!

² Thou hast given him his heart's desire, and hast not withholden the request of his lips. Selah.

³ For thou preventest him with the blessings of goodness: thou settest a crown of pure gold on his head.

⁴ He asked life of thee, and thou gavest it him, even length of days for ever and ever.

⁵ His glory is great in thy salvation: honour and majesty hast thou laid upon him.

Psalms for Overcoming Enemies

WHEN ENEMIES SEEM OVERWHELMING

*Y*ou are your own worst enemy or your own best friend. Others can be your enemies only if you attribute more power to them than is due. Scripture tells us to "fret not ourselves because of evil doers, neither be thy envious against the workers of iniquity for they shall soon be cut down like the grass and wither as the green herb." (Psalm 37:1, 2) We are instructed to "trust in the Lord, and do good." (Psalm 37:3) If there are persons who want to subdue you or hinder your progress, pray that you can rise above their enmity and read Psalm 70: 1–5.

PSALM 70
Verses 1–5

¹ Make haste, O God to deliver me; make haste to help me, O Lord.

² Let them be ashamed and confounded that seek after my soul: let them be turned backward, and put to confusion, that desire my hurt.

³ Let them be turned back for a reward of their shame that say, Aha, aha.

⁴ Let all those that seek thee rejoice and be glad in thee: and let such as love thy salvation say continually, Let God be magnified.

⁵ But I am poor and needy: make haste unto me, O God: thou art my help and my deliverer; O Lord, make no tarrying.

WHEN UNHAPPY WITH FAMILY MEMBERS

*T*hose closest to you may seem to make you the unhappiest. This is because they know your strengths and your weaknesses. Jealousy can also plague families; sibling rivalry is common. God's gifts and graces are not the same for everyone, even within a family. Therefore, when jealousy gets the better of family members, the good that they would do and can do, often they will not do. If one close to you causes you grief and unhappiness, pray that God will give you a clean heart and read Psalm 84: 9–10 and Psalm 85: 8.

PSALM 84
Verses 9–10

[9] Behold, O God our shield, and look upon the face of thine anointed.

[10] For a day in thy courts is better than a thousand. I had rather be a doorkeeper in the house of my God, then to dwell in the tents of wickedness.

PSALM 85
Verse 8

[8] I will hear what God the Lord will speak: for he will speak peace unto his people, and to his saints: but let them not turn again to folly.

WHEN CONFRONTED WITH A LEGAL MATTER

Verses 1 and 26–27 of Psalm 35 call for God to plead your case on your behalf. While there is more than one way to look at any issue, God can help those deciding the case to see it from your point of view. In the courtroom, God's divine power can make you, and those representing you, better able to focus on the truth of the facts, without allowing others to distract or derail you. In this way, God works through you to help those who are deciding the verdict to see the truth.

PSALM 35
Verses 1, 26–27

¹ Plead my cause, O Lord, with them that strive with me: fight against them that fight against me.

²⁶ Let them be ashamed and brought to confusion together that rejoice at mine hurt: let them be clothed with shame and dishonour that magnify themselves against me.

²⁷ Let them shout for joy, and be glad, that favour my righteous cause: yea, let them say continually, Let the Lord be magnified, which hath pleasure in the prosperity of his servant.

WHEN INVOLVED IN DIVORCE

Divorce from one who has been a part of your life is difficult. Nevertheless, at times, to separate seems to be the only solution to a bad situation. Some unions are not marriages ordained by God; thus there is no peace. If you have been wronged in your marriage, as you seek to terminate it, carry no hostility in your heart, or you will remain bound. Rather, "Pray for them which despitefully use you, and persecute you" (Matthew 5:44). Also read Psalm 34, verse 14; Psalm 37, verse 3; and Psalm 27, verses 1–2, 13–14, and in that order.

PSALM 34
Verse 14

¹⁴ Depart from evil, and do good; seek peace, and pursue it.

PSALM 37
Verse 3

³ Trust in the Lord, and do good; so shalt thou dwell in the land, and verily thou shalt be fed.

PSALM 27
Verses 1–2, 13–14

¹ The Lord is my light and my salvation; whom shall I fear? the Lord is the strength of my life; of whom shall I be afraid?

² When the wicked, even mine enemies and my foes, came upon me to eat up my flesh, they stumbled and fell.

¹³ I had fainted, unless I had believed to see the goodness of the Lord in the land of the living.

[14] Wait on the Lord: be of good courage, and he shall strengthen thine heart: wait, I say, on the Lord.

WHEN UNCERTAIN ABOUT WHOM TO TRUST

Sometimes it is hard to discern who is trustworthy, but there is one for whom our trust and allegiance are always due. When in doubt, seek the guidance of the Holy Spirit. Then trust in the Lord with all thine heart; and lean not unto thine own understanding. (Proverbs 3:5) The Divine Helper will make clear to you who are your friends and who are your adversaries. Look to your creator and read Psalm 121.

PSALM 121
Verses 1–8

¹ I will lift up mine eyes unto the hills, from whence cometh my help?

² My help cometh from the Lord, which made heaven and earth.

³ He will not suffer thy foot to be moved; he that keepeth thee will not slumber.

⁴ Behold, he that keepeth Israel shall neither slumber nor sleep.

⁵ The Lord is thy keeper: the Lord is thy shade upon thy right hand.

⁶ The sun shall not smite thee by day, nor the moon by night.

⁷ The Lord shall preserve thee from all evil: he shall preserve thy soul.

⁸ The Lord shall preserve thy going out and thy coming in from this time forth, and even for evermore.

Psalms for Finding True Love

To Meet the Right Person

A person attracts to himself or herself that which he or she is. What determines the "right" person is whether or not he or she is compatible with you. Humans are continually changing, and many fear that the one who is compatible today may not be tomorrow. But if you remain steadfast with God—at the core of your being—then you can trust in the Lord to help you both grow in ways that remain complementary. Read Psalm 34:7 and 8.

PSALM 34
Verses 7–8

7 The angel of the Lord encampeth round about them that fear him, and delivereth them.

8 O taste and see that the Lord is good: blessed is the man that trusteth in him.

To Feel Unafraid to Try Again

If you have been hurt in a love relationship—or several relationships—you may be reluctant to try again. Pray the Lord continues to have mercy upon you and will restore to you the joy of God's salvation. Pray that God will replace in you the free spirit of your youth. Refer to Psalm 126: 1–6.

PSALM 126
Verses 1–6

¹ When the Lord turned again the captivity of Zion, we were like them that dream.

² Then was our mouth filled with laughter, and our tongue with singing: then said they among the heathen, The Lord hath done great things for them.

³ The Lord hath done great things for us; whereof we are glad.

⁴ Turn again our captivity, O Lord, as the streams in the south.

⁵ They that sow in tears shall reap in joy.

⁶ He that goeth forth and weepeth, bearing precious seed, shall doubtless come again with rejoicing, bringing his sheaves with him.

To Feel Unafraid to Trust

There is a difference in being unafraid to try to have a relationship again and being able to trust once you become involved. Learn to trust only in God. Appreciate the words of the Lord that say "Cursed be the man that trusteth in man, and maketh flesh his arm, and whose heart departeth from the Lord." (Jeremiah 17:15) Trust God and you will be free to trust any relationship brought into existence by God's creation. Read Psalm 146:3 and Psalm 105:4.

PSALM 146
Verse 3

³ Put not your trust in princes, nor in the son of man, in whom there is no help.

PSALM 105
Verse 4

⁴ Seek the Lord, and his strength: seek his face evermore.

To Reconcile a Broken Relationship

Estrangement from someone you love comes when you forget to love him or her as you love yourself. Always make the same allowance for the wrongful acts of another as you do for your own wrongful acts. Often we pray "forgive us our debts as we forgive those who our debtors." Yet we are not willing to forgive others. How many times has God forgiven you? When you love another, you are able to forgive as many times as God has forgiven you. With forgiveness, no relationship can remain broken. Forget false pride; yield to Divine Guidance and be happy. Read Psalm 103:1–3; Psalm 86:3–5; and Psalm 85:2–3.

PSALM 103
Verses 1–3

¹ Bless the Lord, O my soul: and all that is within me, bless his holy name.

² Bless the Lord, O my soul, and forget not all his benefits:

³ Who forgiveth all thine iniquities; who healeth all thy diseases;

PSALM 86
Verses 3–5

³ Be merciful unto me, O Lord: for I cry unto thee daily.

⁴ Rejoice the soul of thy servant: for unto thee, O Lord, do I lift up my soul.

⁵ For thou, Lord, art good, and ready to forgive; and plenteous in mercy unto all them that call upon thee.

PSALM 85
Verses 2–3

[2] Thou hast forgiven the iniquity of thy people, thou hast covered all their sin. Selah.

[3] Thou hast taken away all thy wrath: thou hast turned thyself from the fierceness of thine anger.

To Accept Another's Weakness

One sure way to accept another's weakness is to realize that anything another does, you would also do given the same set of circumstance, the same frame of mind, and the same time and place. In Psalm 139, verses 1–10, we are reminded that everything we have is from God. We know that, without God, we also are frail.

PSALM 139
Verses 1–10

¹ O Lord, thou hast searched me, and known me.

² Thou knowest my downsitting and mine uprising, thou understandest my thought afar off.

³ Thou compassest my path and my lying down, and art acquainted with all my ways.

⁴ For there is not a word in my tongue, but, lo, O Lord, thou knowest it altogether.

⁵ Thou hast beset me behind and before, and laid thine hand upon me.

⁶ Such knowledge is too wonderful for me; it is high, I cannot attain unto it.

⁷ Whither shall I go from thy spirit? or whither shall I flee from thy presence?

⁸ If I ascend up into heaven, thou art there: if I made my bed in hell, behold, thou art there.

⁹ If I take the wings of the morning, and dwell in the uttermost parts of the sea;

¹⁰ Even there shall thy hand lead me, and thy right hand shall hold me.

WHEN DECIDING TO MARRY

" . . . *F*aith, hope, and love, . . . but the greatest of these is love" (I Corinthians 13:13). Marriage should be the capstone of human love. When you decide to marry, you will not enter into it lightly. Marriage is a Holy Estate instituted by God. Therefore, to be happy in marriage, your spiritual growth must remain paramount. If you seek God first and place God at the head of your household, your marriage will bring you manifold blessings and your house will be a home. See Psalm 127: 1.

PSALM 127
Verse 1

[1] Except the Lord build the house, they labour in vain that build it: except the Lord keep the city, the watchman waketh but in vain.

Psalms for Gaining Confidence

To Have Courage

Courage allows you to attune yourself to the indwelling spirit of God and to realize your true self. All good endeavors sustain the spirit of God. There is no need to fear. Regardless of the odds, if you are pursuing right, you can be assured of victory. Know that if God is for you, it counts more than the whole world being against you. No one can gain optimum courage without doing right and wholly trusting in God, who is always on the side of right. To help you gain courage refer often to Psalm 27, verse 1.

PSALM 27
Verse 1

¹ The Lord is my light and my salvation; whom shall I fear? the Lord is the strength of my life; of whom shall I be afraid?

WHEN MEETING OTHERS

*Y*ou lack confidence to meet other people when you see others as giants and yourself as a grasshopper. But all creatures are made in God's spiritual image. Therefore, if you are reluctant to meet others, meet them first on a spiritual level. Let the God in you love the God in them and the friendship will easily follow. Remember all of humanity is encumbered by brokenness. The person you are trying to get the confidence to meet is probably trying to get the confidence to meet you. Never be shaken by another's overt appearance of self-assurance. See Psalm 31:1, 23–24.

PSALM 31
Verses 1, 23–24

¹ In thee, O Lord, do I put my trust; let me never be ashamed: deliver me in thy righteousness.

²³ O love the Lord, all ye his saints: for the Lord preserveth the faithful, and plentifully rewardeth the proud doer.

²⁴ Be of good courage, and he shall strengthen your heart, all ye that hope in the Lord.

IN PUBLIC SPEAKING

*W*hen you are called upon to speak in public, remember that since the tongue has the ability to give life or to give death, every speech should give life. When your purpose in speaking is to give life, your confidence increases and you are anointed from on high. Mighty forces come to rescue you from any anxiety. You become a messenger for God and God is right there with you. Before you speak, read Psalm 38:21–22; Psalm 19:14.

PSALM 38
Verses 21–22

[21] Forsake me not, O Lord: O my God, be not far from me.

[22] Make haste to help me, O Lord my salvation.

PSALM 19
Verse 14

[14] Let the words of my mouth, and the meditation of my heart, be acceptable in thy sight, O Lord, my strength, and my redeemer.

AT WORK

*M*ost jobs are demanding. There are always tasks to be performed, goals to be reached, deadlines to be met. It is easy to lose confidence in your ability. Always remember: You are only responsible for doing your best. Only one boss really matters, and you and your supervisor are both accountable. Insecurity can creep in when you feel that the money needed for basic necessities is somehow associated with your job performance. God is the supplier of all your needs. Trust God. After you have done your best, rest in the fairness of a just God. When you feel overwhelmed, see Psalm 111:2–6.

PSALM 111
Verses 2–6

² The works of the Lord are great, sought out of all them that have pleasure therein.

³ His work is honourable and glorious: and his righteousness endureth for ever.

⁴ He hath made his wonderful works to be remembered: the Lord is gracious and full of compassion.

⁵ He hath given meat unto them that fear him: he will ever be mindful of his covenant.

⁶ He hath shewed his people the power of his works, that he may give them the heritage of the heathen.

WITHIN MARRIAGE

A wonderful marriage is a blessing from God and should be looked at as such. An unhappy marriage is demoralizing. No good marriage can occur unless both parties have confidence in God and in each other. Confidence within a marriage can be gained by the parties praying together, reading the Bible together, and becoming friends so that each can rest in the full joy of the Lord. Read Psalm 128.

PSALM 128
Verses 1–6

[1] Blessed is every one that feareth the Lord; that walketh in his ways.

[2] For thou shalt eat the labour of thine hands: happy shalt thou be, and it shall be well with thee.

[3] Thy wife shall be as a fruitful vine by the sides of thine house: thy children like olive plants round about thy table.

[4] Behold, that thus shall the man be blessed that feareth the Lord.

[5] The Lord shall bless thee out of Zion: and thou shalt see the good of Jerusalem all the days of thy life.

[6] Yea, thou shalt see thy children's children, and peace upon Israel.

WHILE RAISING CHILDREN

*C*hildren are gifts from God. No opportunity to be meaningfully with your children is too small or insignificant for you to take full advantage of it. The hours you spend transporting children, riding in elevators, standing in lines, and doing the myriad daily tasks children require: all are opportunities to show love. So that your children can grow up with a sense of integrity and love in their hearts, help them learn to enjoy being alone in the presence of God. As parents, your constant communion with God will show them the way and will help you have the confidence needed to rear your children properly. Read Psalm 78:4–7 constantly as you let go and let God take control of your children's lives.

PSALM 78
Verses 4–7

⁴ We will not hide them from their children, shewing to the generation to come the praises of the Lord, and his strength, and his wonderful works that he hath done.

⁵ For he established a testimony in Jacob, and appointed a law in Israel, which he commanded our fathers, that they should make them known to their children.

⁶ That the generation to come might know them, even the children which should be born; who should arise and declare them to their children.

⁷ That they might set their hope in God, and not forget the works of God, but keep his commandments.

WHEN EXPERIENCING NEGATIVE FEELINGS

*I*nevitably, negative feelings will invade your spirit. Harboring such feelings is detrimental to your health. But so is pretending they are not there. Accept negative feelings, but also find a means to release them. You need confidence in order to express the negative feelings in a way that does not harm others. Negative thinking should only be given speech after much prayer. Actively seek the way. To hold the feelings in—or to misuse them in some way—is to allow yourself to be oppressed. Ask God to deliver your soul from feelings of hostility. Read Psalm 142, verse 7, as God begins to set you free for positive thinking.

PSALM 142
Verse 7

7 Bring my soul out of prison, that I may praise
thy name: the righteous shall compass me about;
for thou shalt deal bountifully with me.

WHEN REVEALING DEEP FEELINGS

*I*f you have experienced rejection, you may shy away from expressing deep feelings. However, many blessed opportunities may escape you if you hesitate to give tongue to the magnitude of your feelings. The world is hungry for manifestations of deep feelings of love. If you need confidence to express what you feel, read Psalm 144, verse 9.

PSALM 144
Verse 9

⁹ I will sing a new song unto thee, O God: upon
a psaltery and an instrument of ten strings will I
sing praises unto thee.

WHEN ASKING FORGIVENESS

Sometimes you act out of frustration, anger, depression, and despair. Sometimes actions or words cause misunderstanding, heartbreak, disappointment, and they can inflame the emotions of others. In order to rectify the situation, you must ask forgiveness. Confidence usually comes when you can face your own shortcomings and share with another the experience that prompted the rage. When you meditate on Psalm 51:1 and 10, the struggle within usually subsides.

PSALM 51
Verses 1, 10

¹ Have mercy upon me, O God, according to thy lovingkindness: according unto the multitude of thy tender mercies blot out my trangressions.

¹⁰ Create in me a clean heart, O God; and renew a right spirit within me.

WHEN OFFERING FORGIVENESS TO OTHERS

*T*he act of forgiveness is a manifestation of love—love of self, love of God, and love of humanity. Forgiveness is a spiritual opportunity. True forgiveness must be accompanied by forgetfulness. Just as we ask God to throw our sins into a sea of forgetfulness, we should likewise throw the wrongful acts of others into the same place. Staying tied to the past aborts future potential. See Psalm 51:12–15.

PSALM 51
Verses 12–15

¹² Restore unto me the joy of thy salvation; and uphold me with thy free spirit.

¹³ Then will I teach transgressors thy ways; and sinners shall be converted unto thee.

¹⁴ Deliver me from bloodguiltiness, O God, thou God of my salvation: and my tongue shall sing aloud of thy righteousness.

¹⁵ O Lord, open thou my lips; and my mouth shall shew forth thy praise.

WHEN SEARCHING FOR A FRIEND

A true friend loves at all times. But a true friend is a rare find. Whether searching for a lost friend or for one you have not met, do not be discouraged. First, realize you have a steadfast friend in God who loves at all times and bears all your faults. When searching for a friend, read Psalm 119, verse 63.

PSALM 119
Verse 63

[63] I am a companion of all them that fear thee, and of them that keep thy precepts.

Psalms for Coping with Emotions

WHEN FEELING GENERAL FEAR

*F*ear is faith that has lost its way. You do not need to be a victim of fear. When the feeling of fear overwhelms you and you are left trembling because of impending danger—real or imagined—empty your mind of all but the love of God. Take your concerns to God on a daily basis, and leave them there. God will give ear to your prayers and save you. Put your trust in Almighty God, read the words of Psalms 55:22 and believe. Fear will be replaced with faith, peace, and self assurance.

PSALM 55
Verse 22

²² Cast thy burden upon the Lord, and he shall sustain thee: he shall never suffer the righteous to be moved.

WHEN FEELING FEAR OF AGING

*T*here comes a time when the flesh ceases to be firm and smooth, when the mind is not quite as alert as it once was, the teeth are not as sound, the sight grows dim, and the body loses its agility. No one, except through an early entrance to the grave, is completely spared this process.

Degeneration of the body should be accompanied with regeneration of the soul. For those who see the slowing of the body as an opportunity to rest and meditate on spiritual things, the aging process is accepted with much gratitude. If you find yourself feeling fear of aging, read Psalm 37:25.

PSALM 37
Verse 25

25 I have been young, and now am old; yet have I not seen the righteous forsaken, nor his seed begging bread.

WHEN FEELING FEAR OF DEATH

*D*eath is common to all living creatures. However, precious in the sight of the Lord is the death of his saints. Blessed are those who die believing that to be able to rest from all labor is a reward; who anticipate a new life forever in the presence of God. God will be with you even as you make this eternal transformation. Thus, you go to the grave, not frightened, but faithful. See Psalm 23:4.

PSALM 23
Verse 4

⁴ Yea, though I walk through the valley of the shadow of death, I will fear no evil: for thou art with me; thy rod and thy staff they comfort me.

WHEN FEELING ANXIETY

*M*ost people suffer from anxiety and uneasiness because they trouble themselves over events and situations that should not be their worries. We try to fix things for others that only they themselves or God can fix; or we are in a hurry to get things done *our* way. *Wait patiently for the Lord.* (Psalm 40:1) If you can learn to wait on the Lord you will see in due time that that which caused you anxiety dissipates as a mist. God will lead you in truth and teach you the ways of righteousness. When you consider God's power to heal, to create, to make right the wrongs, you relax because you rest in God—who can do everything except fail. Read Psalm 27, verses 4–5, 8, and 13–14, when anxiety threatens to overwhelm you.

PSALM 27
Verses 4–5, 8, 13–14

4 One thing have I desired of the Lord, that will I seek after; that I may dwell in the house of the Lord all the days of my life, to behold the beauty of the Lord, and to inquire in his temple.

5 For in the time of trouble he shall hide me in his pavilion: in the secret of his tabernacle shall he hide me; he shall set me up upon a rock.

8 When thou saidst, Seek ye my face; my heart said unto thee, Thy face, Lord, will I seek.

13 I had fainted, unless I had believed to see the goodness of the Lord in the land of the living.

14 Wait on the Lord: be of good courage, and he shall strengthen thine heart: wait, I say, on the Lord.

WHEN FEELING STRESS

Though usually brought on by external forces, stress, if allowed unguarded access, can do much harm to your mind, body, and spirit. Therefore, it is important that it be brought into check as soon as possible. This process can be facilitated by simply taking time to count your blessings. An "attitude of gratitude" has been proven to relieve stress. Pause and read Psalm 119: 33–40.

PSALM 119
Verses 33–40

³³ Teach me, O Lord, the way of thy statutes; and I shall keep it unto the end.

³⁴ Give me understanding, and I shall keep thy law; yea, I shall observe it with my whole heart.

³⁵ Make me to go in the path of thy commandments; for therein do I delight.

³⁶ Incline my heart unto thy testimonies, and not to covetousness.

³⁷ Turn away mine eyes from beholding vanity; and quicken thou me in thy way.

³⁸ Stablish thy word unto thy servant, who is devoted to thy fear.

³⁹ Turn away my reproach which I fear: for thy judgments are good.

⁴⁰ Behold, I have longed after thy precepts: quicken me in thy righteousness.

WHEN FEELING OVERWHELMED

*I*n this high-pressured, commercialized, global, and automated society, it has become almost natural to feel overwhelmed. It seems that even when we strive to walk in righteousness, we are battered from all sides by those who are more worldly. It is no wonder you feel bewildered. But do not be discouraged. Meditate on the word of God and continue to watch. You will see those who depend on worldly treasures—those who were once towering over others—wither like cut grass. Psalm 125 brings safety to those who trust in God. It is a prayer for the godly against the wicked.

PSALM 125
Verses 1–5

¹ They that trust in the Lord shall be as mount Zion, which cannot be removed, but abideth for ever.

² As the mountains are round about Jerusalem, so the Lord is round about his people from henceforth even for ever.

³ For the rod of the wicked shall not rest upon the lot of the righteous; lest the righteous put forth their hands unto iniquity.

⁴ Do good, O Lord, unto those that be good, and to them that are upright in their hearts.

⁵ As for such as turn aside unto their crooked ways, the Lord shall lead them forth with the workers of iniquity: but peace shall be upon Israel.

WHEN FEELING DISAPPOINTMENT

*E*veryone experiences disappointment at one time or another. However, disappointment is like a stumbling block; if you don't see it for what it is, it will cause you to fall. But if you recognize it, you can stand on it and use it to reach higher ground. When your best laid plays go awry, submit yourself and your plans to God. Then rest in the Lord. If things do not follow your expectations, realize that "the mind of man plans his path, but the Lord directs his steps." (Proverbs 16:9) Begin to look and see what other avenues the Lord is opening to you. See Psalm 17:8 and Psalm 16:1.

PSALM 17
Verse 8

⁸ Keep me as the apple of the eye, hide me under the shadow of thy wings. . . .

PSALM 16
Verse 1

¹ Preserve me, O God: for in thee do I put my trust.

WHEN FEELING GUILT

*A*ll have done wrong for which the remembrance grieves our spirits and causes us to mourn. We regret the past and languish in self pity. But to feel ashamed for wrong is a good thing. It means you have not lost sight of the eternal values. Likewise, guilt is the first step toward repentance. God is always willing to have mercy on you. Confess your wrongdoing before God and ask that your joy be restored. Read Psalm 51:14.

PSALM 51
Verse 14

[14] Deliver me from bloodguiltiness, O God, thou God of my salvation: and my tongue shall sing aloud of thy righteousness.

WHEN FEELING REGRET

*I*f you feel remorseful for things you have thought, said, or done, and you wish to relieve another of the grief that you have caused, cry first to the Lord. Ask that God cleanse you and seek forgiveness. Regret is only the first step. When you repent and make amends you use regret as a stepping stone to a higher level. See Psalm 44: 15–21, 23, and 26, and Psalm 45:6.

PSALM 44
Verses 15–21, 23, 26

¹⁵ My confusion is continually before me, and the shame of my face hath covered me,

¹⁶ For the voice of him that reproacheth and blasphemeth; by reason of the enemy and avenger.

¹⁷ All this is come upon us; yet have we not forgotten thee, neither have we dealt falsely in thy covenant.

¹⁸ Our heart is not turned back neither have our steps declined from thy way;

¹⁹ Though thou hast sore broken us in the place of dragons, and covered us with the shadow of death.

²⁰ If we have forgotten the name of our God, or stretched out our hands to a strange god;

²¹ Shall not God search this out? for he knoweth the secrets of the heart.

²³ Awake, why sleepest thou, O Lord? arise, cast us not off for ever.

²⁶ Arise for our help, and redeem us for thy mercies' sake.

PSALM 45
Verse 6

⁶ Thy throne, O God, is for ever and ever: the sceptre of thy kingdom is a right sceptre.

WHEN FEELING SADNESS

*I*t is natural to feel sadness when specific events assail you. There is a time to mourn and a time to weep. When you embrace sadness and let it carry you through grief and sorrow, know that eventually you must give your sadness to the Lord. If you allow the feelings to overcome you, you will become depressed and unable to hear the voice of God giving you reason to rejoice again. When sadness comes, read Psalm 21: 1–4, Psalm 17: 17–18, and Psalm 63:3. Afterward, take your attention off yourself and your situation and give your attention to God and to others.

PSALM 21
Verses 1–4

¹ The king shall joy in thy strength, O Lord; and in thy salvation how greatly shall he rejoice!

² Thou hast given him his heart's desire, and hast not withholden the request of his lips. Selah.

³ For thou preventest him with the blessings of goodness: thou settest a crown of pure gold on his head.

⁴ He asked life of thee, and thou gavest it him, even length of days for ever and ever.

PSALM 17
Verses 7–8

⁷ Shew thy marvellous lovingkindness, O thou that savest by thy right hand them which put their trust in thee from those that rise up against them.

⁸ Keep me as the apple of the eye, hide me under the shadow of thy wings,

PSALM 63
Verse 3

³ Because thy lovingkindness is better than life, my lips shall praise thee.

WHEN FEELING LONELY

To be without friends, companionship, or associates may cause you to feel lonely. But if you learn to use this time as time to praise God, you will be blessed with God's companionship. You can also feel lonely in a crowd of friends if you have not taken time to be alone with God so that you know, always, whose you are. When you are constantly in the company of others, even those who feed your spirit, you lose opportunities to go one-on-one with God. When feeling lonely, see—in this order—Psalm 88:1, 18, and 2; and Psalm 89: 5–18.

PSALM 88
Verses 1, 18, 2

¹ O Lord God of my salvation, I have cried day and night before thee.

¹⁸ Lover and friend hast thou put far from me, and mine acquaintance into darkness.

² Let my prayer come before thee: incline thine ear unto my cry;

PSALM 89
Verses 5–18

⁵ And the heavens shall praise thy wonders, O Lord: thy faithfulness also in the congregation of the saints.

⁶ For who in the heaven can be compared unto the Lord? who among the sons of the mighty can be likened unto the Lord?

⁷ God is greatly to be feared in the assembly of the saints, and to be had in reverence of all them that are about him.

⁸ O Lord God of hosts, who is a strong Lord like unto thee? or to thy faithfulness round about thee?

⁹ Thou rulest the raging of the sea: when the waves thereof arise, thou stillest them.

¹⁰ Thou hast broken Rahab in pieces, as one that is slain; thou hast scattered thine enemies with thine strong arm,

¹¹ The heavens are thine, the earth also is thine: as for the world and the fulness thereof, thou hast founded them.

¹² The north and the south, thou hast created them: Tabor and Hermon shall rejoice in thy name.

¹³ Thou hast a mighty arm: strong is thy hand, and high is thy right hand.

¹⁴ Justice and judgment are the habitation of thy throne: mercy and truth shall go before thy face.

¹⁵ Blessed is the people that know the joyful sound: they shall walk, O Lord, in the light of thy countenance.

¹⁶ In thy name shall they rejoice all the day: and in thy righteousness shall they be exalted.

¹⁷ For thou art the glory of their strength: and in thy favour our horn shall be exalted.

¹⁸ For the Lord is our defence; and the Holy One of Israel is our king.

WHEN FEELING IMPATIENCE

*J*ust as the Lord has had patience with you, you are called to have patience with others. Without perpetual hope, long-suffering with patience becomes impossible. And you must also be patient with God, whose timetable is not your timetable, but who knows best when to give you your heart's desire. When it seems that your human patience is at an end and your repeated requests of the Lord have not materialized, Psalm 37:34 should be your stronghold.

PSALM 37
Verse 34

[34] Wait on the Lord, and keep his way, and he shall exalt thee to inherit the land: when the wicked are cut off, thou shalt see it.

WHEN NEEDING TOLERANCE

*A*s with patience, everyone has a different level of tolerance. The particular way you were created allows you to tolerate more heat or more cold than another; or more noise or solitude than another. Some people are more tolerant of differences in others, as well. If you need more tolerance toward the uniqueness of other human beings, then pause and think that as different as you are from them, they are that different from you. Thus they have to tolerate your differences in the same degree that you are tolerating theirs. See Psalm 31: 1–5.

PSALM 31
Verses 1–5

[1] In thee, O Lord, do I put my trust; let me never be ashamed: deliver me in thy righteousness.

[2] Bow down thine ear to me; deliver me speedily: be thou my strong rock, for an house of defense to save me.

[3] For thou art my rock and my fortress; therefore for thy name's sake lead me, and guide me.

[4] Pull me out of the net that they have laid privily for me: for thou art my strength.

[5] Into thine hand I commit my spirit: thou hast redeemed me, O Lord God of truth.

Psalms for Relief from Suffering

❧

FROM CONTINUOUS PAIN

*I*f you are in continuous pain, you suffer much. Perhaps you even want to approach God in a spirit of indignation and ask, like the prophet Jeremiah, "Why is my pain perpetual, and my wound incurable that refuses to be healed?" (Jeremiah 15:18) Know that God is with you to save and deliver you. Read Psalm 69: 1–3 and Psalm 41: 2–3 and 13 for consolation and healing.

PSALM 69
Verses 1–3

¹ Save me, O God; for the waters are come in unto my soul.

² I sink in deep mire, where there is no standing: I am come into deep waters, where the floods overflow me.

³ I am weary of my crying: my throat is dried: mine eyes fail while I wait for my God.

PSALM 41
Verses 2–3, 13

² The Lord will preserve him, and keep him alive; and he shall be blessed upon the earth: and thou wilt not deliver him unto the will of his enemies.

³ The Lord will strengthen him upon the bed of languishing: thou wilt make all his bed in his sickness.

¹³ Blessed be the Lord God of Israel from everlasting, and to everlasting. Amen, and Amen.

FOR GRIEF OVER LOST LOVE

*I*f you are distressed because one you admire and find delight in has withdrawn affection from you, say to yourself until convinced, "If you can stand to leave me, I can stand to see you go." Value yourself and treat yourself to what you are worth. Trust God to know what is best for you. Thank God for giving you the opportunity to begin afresh. Let your new beginning start with showing affection for God. Read Psalm 91:14, Psalm 31:23, and Psalm 18:1.

PSALM 91
Verse 14

[14] Because he hath set his love upon me, therefore will I deliver him: I will set him on high, because he hath known my name.

PSALM 31
Verse 23

[23] O love the Lord, all ye his saints: for the Lord preserveth the faithful, and plentifully rewardeth the proud doer.

PSALM 18
Verse 1

[1] I will love thee, O Lord, my strength.

FOR GRIEF OVER UNREQUITED LOVE

*L*ove that is not returned naturally brings grief. It is vanity to continue to suffer because love is not reciprocated. You are angry because you think the one you care for refuses to love you. You become distracted while plotting all the ways to make the relationship work. Yet when you love yourself and understand the ways of God, you realize that love ordained by God flows from one to another without striving. See Psalm 4:2.

PSALM 4
Verse 2

[2] O ye sons of men, how long will ye turn my glory into shame? how long will ye love vanity, and seek [falsehood]! Selah.

For Grief at the Death of a Beloved

$\mathcal{O}$ne reason we grieve at the death of a friend or family member is that we don't understand death. Where has she gone? Why did he have to die? Why must I be left alone? We tie ourselves in knots with these questions. However, if we can submit our will to that of the Lord, at that moment difficulty will subside. We do know that our beloved has no more pain, no more sickness, no more sorrow, no more heartaches or disappointments. They have rest from all labor and are at peace and enjoying a reunion with God. See Psalm 36:5–10 and Psalm 44: 17–19 for relief. Also, when grieving after the death of a loved one, set your love upon the Lord and they will be precious memories that sustain you. (Colossians 3:2) Read Psalm 91: 14–16.

PSALM 36
Verses 5–10

⁵ Thy mercy, O Lord, is in the heavens; and thy faithfulness reacheth unto the clouds.

⁶ Thy righteousness is like the great mountains; thy judgments are a great deep: O Lord, thou preservest man and beast.

⁷ How excellent is thy lovingkindness, O God! therefore the children of men put their trust under the shadow of thy wings.

⁸ They shall be abundantly satisfied with the fatness of thy house; and thou shalt make them drink of the river of thy pleasures.

⁹ For with thee is the fountain of life: in thy light shall we see light.

¹⁰ O continue thy lovingkindness unto them that know thee; and thy righteousness to the upright in heart.

PSALM 44
Verses 17–19

¹⁷ All this is come upon us; yet have we not forgotten thee, neither have we dealt falsely in thy covenant.

¹⁸ Our heart is not turned back neither have our steps declined from thy way;

¹⁹ Though thou hast sore broken us in the place of dragons, and covered us with the shadow of death.

PSALM 91
Verses 14–16

¹⁴ Because he hath set his love upon me, therefore will I deliver him: I will set him on high, because he hath known my name.

¹⁵ He shall call upon me, and I will answer him: I will be with him in trouble; I will deliver him, and honour him.

¹⁶ With long life will I satisfy him, and shew him my salvation.

FOR GRIEF AT THE DEATH OF A PARENT

God is the author of life and death. For each person God has appointed a time to die. God always knows best. However, when parents die we become more aware than ever of our own mortality, and so our grief takes on more significance. We may be frightened and momentarily lose faith in the love and wisdom of God. Ironically, it is by dwelling momentarily on your own mortality—with the knowledge that God's will for you will prevail—that you will most quickly rise from your bed of grief and go on with the life God has given you to live. Read Psalm 103: 1–2, 13–17.

PSALM 103
Verses 1–2, 13–17

[1] Bless the Lord, O my soul: and all that is within me, bless his holy name.

[2] Bless the Lord, O my soul, and forget not all his benefits:

[13] Like as the father pitieth his children, so the Lord pitieth them that fear him.

[14] For he knoweth our frame; he remembereth that we are dust.

[15] As for man, his days are as grass: as a flower of the field, so he flourisheth.

[16] For the wind passeth over it, and it is gone; and the place thereof shall know it no more.

[17] But the mercy of the Lord is from everlasting to everlasting upon them that fear him, and his righteousness unto children's children. . . .

FOR GRIEF AT THE DEATH OF A CHILD

*I*t is natural to assume that a child will outlive the parent. Therefore, when a child precedes a parent in death the sorrow of the whole community is overwhelming. Sometimes the only comfort is in knowing that a lost child resides with the Lord. Read Psalm 102: 1–2, 13, and 27–28.

PSALM 102
Verses 1–2, 13, 27–28

[1] Hear my prayer, O Lord, and let my cry come unto thee.

[2] Hide not thy face from me in the day when I am in trouble; incline thine ear unto me: in the day when I call answer me speedily.

[13] Thou shalt arise, and have mercy upon Zion: for the time to favour her, yea, the set time, is come.

[27] But thou art the same, and thy years shall have no end.

[28] The children of thy servants shall continue, and their seed shall be established before thee.

Psalms for Blessings on Important Occasions

WHEN BEING BAPTIZED

The sacrament of baptism is an outward sign of an inner transformation. It signifies a new birth of spirit. It follows repentance for the remission of sin. The water symbolizes cleansing; the baptized one is cleansed of sins and is ready to accept grace through the Lord God. See Psalm 119:105–106 and 145–149.

PSALM 119
Verses 105–106, 145–149

105 Thy word is a lamp unto my feet, and a light unto my path.

106 I have sworn, and I will perform it, that I will keep thy righteous judgments.

145 I cried with my whole heart; hear me, O Lord: I will keep thy statutes.

146 I cried unto thee; save me, and I shall keep thy testimonies.

147 I prevented the dawning of the morning, and cried: I hoped in thy word.

148 Mine eyes prevent the night watches, that I might meditate in thy word.

149 Hear my voice according unto thy loving-kindness: O Lord, quicken me according to thy judgment.

WHEN GETTING MARRIED

To have the love, compassion, and companionship of a caring spouse is one of God's greatest blessings. To be able to remain in one relationship throughout your life is a goal worth seeking. In a true marriage, the partners will walk together in the spirit. They understand that every marriage should have three parties because they are divinely blessed, and that there should always be room in their home for the God of Love. See Psalm 24:1, 7–8.

PSALM 24
Verses 1, 7–8

[1] The earth is the Lord's, and the fulness thereof; the world, and they that dwell therein.

[7] Lift up your heads, O ye gates; and be ye lift up, ye everlasting doors; and the King of glory shall come in.

[8] Who is this King of glory? The Lord strong and mighty, the Lord mighty in battle.

WHEN CELEBRATING
AN ANNIVERSARY

*A*nniversaries are like pebbles dropped along the way to indicate the path you have traveled. When looked upon as a blessing, an anniversary will help you appreciate your past and will give you a clear vision for the future. As you pause and offer gratitude to God for the journey you have travel and will continue, read Psalm 150.

PSALM 150
Verses 1–6

[1] Praise ye the Lord. Praise God in his sanctuary: praise him in the firmament of his power.

[2] Praise him for his mighty acts: praise him according to his excellent greatness.

[3] Praise him with the sound of the trumpet: praise him with the psaltery and harp.

[4] Praise him with the timbrel and dance: praise him with stringed instruments and organs.

[5] Praise him upon the loud cymbals: praise him upon the high sounding cymbals.

[6] Let every thing that hath breath praise the Lord. Praise ye the Lord.

WHEN CHRISTENING A CHILD

*R*emember constantly that your child comes from God. On the day of his or her christening you give an outward expression of your understanding that you are giving your child back to the creator. The christening also gives you an opportunity to invite your community to help you raise your child according to God's will. As people gather to christen a child, they attest as believers that God can use weak instruments to accomplish great works. Verses 1–4 of Psalm 135 help blessings to flow to this occasion.

PSALM 135
Verses 1–4

[1] Praise ye the Lord. Praise ye the name of the Lord; praise him, O ye servants of the Lord.

[2] Ye that stand in the house of the Lord, in the courts of the house of our God,

[3] Praise the Lord; for the Lord is good: sing praises unto his name; for it is pleasant.

[4] For the Lord hath chosen Jacob unto himself, and Israel for his peculiar treasure.

WHEN GRADUATING

Graduation is an ending and a beginning. It is a time to cherish and celebrate accomplishments, and to reflect in humility on God's great blessings, which have brought you to this point. Pride is never to overtake us. We look toward the future with renewed determination to serve the Lord. To bless the occasion, see Psalm 131:1–3.

PSALM 131
Verses 1–3

[1] Lord, my heart is not haughty, nor mine eyes lofty: neither do I exercise myself in great matters, or in things too high for me.

[2] Surely I have behaved and quieted myself, as a child that is weaned of his mother: my soul is even as a weaned child.

[3] Let Israel hope in the Lord from henceforth and for ever.

WHEN CELEBRATING A BIRTHDAY

*G*od created each of us and is mindful of us every day of our lives. But on every birthday we can take time to savor the anniversary of the day God gave us life. Whether you are young and rising toward life's peaks or older and rising toward eternity, bless each birthday with words from Psalm 8:1, 3–5.

PSALM 8
Verses 1, 3–5

¹ O Lord our Lord, how excellent is thy name in all the earth! who hast set thy glory above the heavens.

³ When I consider thy heavens, the work of thy fingers, the moon and the stars, which thou hast ordained;

⁴ What is man, that thou art mindful of him? and the son of man, that thou visitest him?

⁵ For thou hast made him a little lower than the angels, and hast crowned him with glory and honour.

Psalms for Happiness

For Allowing Oneself to Experience Joy

*I*n God's presence the fullness of joy comes. When we go for too long a time without intentionally centering on the presence of God, we can become captives of anger, hopelessness, and fear. When we adorn ourselves in frivolities, we become hypocrites to ourselves. Happiness thus achieved camouflages true joy. When you leave material considerations behind and center yourself before God, you will be shown the pathway to joy. When life sends a trial, you will understand that it is only momentary. Thus, you can pass through the storms of life knowing unspeakable joy while you look for the light shining in the darkness. See Psalm 43, verse 4, and Psalm 100.

PSALM 43
Verse 4

⁴ Then will I go unto the altar of God, unto God my exceeding joy: yea, upon the harp will I praise thee, O God my God.

PSALM 100
Verses 1–5

¹ Make a joyful noise unto the Lord, all ye lands.

² Serve the Lord with gladness: come before his presence with singing.

³ Know ye that the Lord he is God: it is he that hath made us, and not we ourselves; we are his people, and the sheep of his pasture.

⁴ Enter into his gates with thanksgiving, and into his courts with praise: be thankful unto him, and bless his name.

⁵ For the Lord is good; his mercy endureth to all generations.

FOR APPRECIATING WHAT ONE HAS

*I*t is sad to have everything and appreciate nothing. Goods unjustly acquired can never be appreciated by the one who has obtained them. The acquisition of material goods for vain purposes will never be enough. If we think what we have gained is through our own will and more can only be gained through our own efforts, then striving will be perpetual and true satisfaction and enjoyment will never come. When we realize the earth is the Lord's and it is only through the grace of God that we have any part of it, then we can live in appreciation of what God has so graciously allowed us to use. Read Psalm 39:6-8 and Psalm 20:6-7.

PSALM 39
Verse 6–8

⁶ Surely every man walketh in a vain shew: surely they are disquieted in vain: he heapeth up riches, and knoweth not who shall gather them.

⁷ And now, Lord, what wait I for? my hope is in thee.

⁸ Deliver me from all my transgressions: make me not the reproach of the foolish.

PSALM 20
Verses 6–7

⁶ Now know I that the Lord saveth his anointed; he will hear him from his holy heaven with the saving strength of his right hand,

⁷ Some trust in chariots, and some in horses: but we will remember the name of the Lord our God.

FOR LIVING IN THE MOMENT

*R*egrets, anger, guilt, and fear cause us to linger in the past or rush with anxious anticipation toward the future. Yet happiness lies neither in the past nor in contemplating the future. To find happiness, take the time to savor the moment. Acknowledge a cool breeze, the shuffle of a wave, the falling of a leaf, the delicious aroma of a cookout, the busyness of an ant, or the stories told in the clouds. Read Psalm 95, verses 1–8, to help you center and appreciate the present moment.

PSALM 95
Verses 1–8

¹ O come, let us sing unto the Lord: let us make a joyful noise to the rock of our salvation.

² Let us come before his presence with thanksgiving, and make a joyful noise unto him with psalms.

³ For the Lord is a great God, and a great King above all gods.

⁴ In his hand are the deep places of the earth: the strength of the hills is his also.

⁵ The sea is his, and he made it: and his hands formed the dry land.

⁶ O come, let us worship and bow down: let us kneel before the Lord our maker.

⁷ For he is our God; and we are the people of his pasture, and the sheep of his hand. Today if ye will hear his voice,

⁸ Harden not your heart, as in the provocation, and as in the day of temptation in the wilderness.

FOR FINDING ONE'S TRUE PATH

Everyone has a Divine Purpose in life. Each person possesses unique talents and gifts to fulfill that purpose. There are several criteria that can be used to help you determine whether you are on your true path. First, if God is for it, you don't have to force it. It flows. Second, you have joy when you are on your true path. And third, you have prosperity when you are on your right path. Everything seems to fall in place. If ever in doubt, be bold. If you are on the right path, mighty forces will come to assist you. For spiritual help, see Psalm 119:133–135. And when you feel you are being led astray by those working against God, read Psalm 118:5–9.

PSALM 119
Verses 133–135

[133] Order my steps in thy word: and let not any iniquity have dominion over me.

[134] Deliver me from the oppression of man: so will I keep thy precepts.

[135] Make thy face to shine upon thy servant; and teach me thy statutes.

PSALM 118
Verses 5–9

[5] I called upon the Lord in distress: the Lord answered me, and set me in a large place.

[6] The Lord is on my side; I will not fear: what can man do unto me?

[7] The Lord taketh my part with them that help me: therefore shall I see my desire upon them that hate me.

[8] It is better to trust in the Lord than to put confidence in man.

[9] It is better to trust in the Lord than to put confidence in princes.

Psalms of Affirmation

❦

FOR INCREASING SELF-DISCIPLINE

Getting self-control requires four basic steps: correct thinking, correct speaking, correct projection of an outcome, and correct action according to your projected vision. If you want self-discipline, ask God and then visualize your desired outcome. Decide that you will no longer throw away God's time as you have in the past. It's a matter of decision and God has placed within you the capacity to make that choice. For an affirmation to increase self-discipline, read Psalm 101:1–3.

PSALM 101
Verses 1–3

¹ I will sing of mercy and judgment: unto thee, O Lord, will I sing.

² I will behave myself wisely in a perfect way. O when wilt thou come unto me? I will walk within my house with a perfect heart.

³ I will set no wicked thing before mine eyes: I hate the work of them that turn aside; it shall not cleave to me.

FOR AFFIRMING ONE'S SUCCESSES

*F*aith-filled thoughts continuously open your consciousness to the divine power that is within you. Scripture says: "If thou canst believe, all things are possible to him that believeth." (Mark 9:23) "What things so ever ye desire, when ye pray, believe that ye receive them, and ye shall have them." (Mark 11:24) "If ye abide in Me, and My words abide in you, ye shall ask what ye will, and it shall be done unto you." (John 15: 7) Today begin speaking of that which is not as if it is, and your success is assured.

"In the beginning was the Word, and the Word was with God, and the Word was God" (John 1:1). Words, spoken in faith, have power. Read Psalm 121:8.

PSALM 121
Verse 8

[8] The Lord shall preserve thy going out and thy coming in from this time forth, and even for evermore.

FOR OVERCOMING FEARS

A certain degree of fear energizes, but unreasonable fear paralyzes. To overcome fear you must completely trust in God. God will keep you in perfect peace if you remember to keep your mind on God. When fearful, read Psalm 27:14 and Psalm 56:3.

PSALM 27
Verse 14

[14] Wait on the Lord: be of good courage, and he shall strengthen thine heart: wait, I say, on the Lord.

PSALM 56
Verse 3

[3] What time I am afraid, I will trust in thee.

FOR AFFIRMING FAITH

*A*n affirmation is a positive form of prayer. It can stimulate you inwardly and then manifest positive action. Affirming your faith can cause you to feel close to God and to experience the magnificence of God: the power and the glory. To continuously affirm your faith, memorize and repeat throughout the day one or all of the following: Psalm 25:1, Psalm 9:1–2, Psalm 18:2, and Psalm 34:1– 2.

PSALM 25
Verse 1

[1] Unto thee, O Lord, do I lift up my soul.

PSALM 9
Verses 1–2

[1] I will praise thee, O Lord, with my whole heart:
I will shew forth all thy marvellous works.

[2] I will be glad and rejoice in thee: I will sing
praise to thy name, O thou most High.

PSALM 18
Verse 2

[2] The Lord is my rock, and my fortress, and my
deliverer; my God, my strength, in whom I will
trust; my buckler, and the horn of my salvation,
and my high tower.

PSALM 34
Verses 1–2

[1] I will bless the Lord at all times: his praise shall continually be in my mouth.

[2] My soul shall make her boast in the Lord: the humble shall hear thereof, and be glad.

WHEN FEELING SELF-DOUBT

*O*vercoming self-doubt requires practice. Establish a routine of recalling past accomplishments. See yourself as you were in your moments of success. Affirm that you still have the same life, the same energy, and the same vitality to do even greater things. See yourself as being wonderfully made in God's image. Thus you can do all things. Psalm 8: 4–9.

PSALM 8
Verses 4–9

4 What is man, that thou art mindful of him? and the son of man, that thou visitest him?

5 For thou hast made him a little lower than the angels, and hast crowned him with glory and honour.

6 Thou madest him to have dominion over the works of thy hands; thou hast put all things under his feet;

7 All sheep and oxen, yea, and the beasts of the field;

8 The fowl of the air, and the fish of the sea, and whatsoever passeth through the paths of the seas.

9 O Lord our Lord, how excellent is thy name in all the earth!

Psalms for Finding Guidance

~⁊~

WHEN RAISING CHILDREN

To be entrusted by the Almighty God with the responsibility of rearing a child represents an awesome responsibility, a great honor, and a profound privilege. While rising to meet the challenge, there will be certain periods when your wisdom will fail you. When emotions run high and situations go out of your control, it will seem to take supernatural strength to handle them. Seek guidance from God, who gave you the task(s). Know that God will not give you more than you can manage. Read Psalm 53:2 and Psalm 54:1–2.

PSALM 53
Verse 2

² God looked down from heaven upon the children of men, to see if there were any that did understand, that did seek God.

PSALM 54
Verses 1–2

¹ Save me, O God, by thy name, and judge me by thy strength.

² Hear my prayer, O God; give ear to the words of my mouth.

WHEN HELPING A FRIEND

*W*hen a friend is in emotional trouble or in physical distress, you can help most by leading that friend to the source of all wisdom, power, and strength. Let her know that you will stand beside her, but that she alone can get the help she needs. She can never hide herself from herself. Only she and God know exactly what she needs. Standing patiently beside her, help her face her trouble directly, and invoke the spirit of the living God to guide her. Read Psalm 119:63.

PSALM 119
Verse 63

63 I am a companion of all them that fear thee,
and of them that keep thy precepts.

WHEN ADVISING ANOTHER

*T*hose who are well advised gain wisdom. Before advising another, remember the words that Jesus said: "For where two or three gather together in my name, there am I in the midst of them." (Matthew 18:20) Always pray before giving advice in order that the words of your mouth and the meditation of your heart will be acceptable to God. Then wait until you hear that still, small voice and know that you have received Divine Illumination. See Psalm 25:5 and Psalm 48:14.

PSALM 25
Verse 5

[5] Lead me in thy truth, and teach me: for thou art the God of my salvation; on thee do I wait all the day.

PSALM 48
Verse 14

[14] For this God is our God for ever and ever: he will be our guide even unto death.

WHEN FACING A MAJOR DECISION

*L*ife offers abundant opportunities for success. To achieve success, however, we often find we have to take risks. Risk might lead to failure. And so major decisions are difficult if we feel we are on our own. It is important to use the knowledge gained from past experiences. If you know what is right, then do that. Otherwise you become like a foolish person who does not know right from wrong. If you are confused about what is right and wrong in a decision you must make, then acknowledge that you are seeing "through a glass darkly." (I Corinthians 13:12) Pray for clarity and read Psalm 25:9.

PSALM 25
Verse 9

⁹ The meek will he guide in judgment: and the meek will he teach his way.

TO HEAR AND TRUST ONE'S OWN
INSTINCTS

*T*here is within us all the inspiration of the Almighty, which gives us understanding. The Lord gives us instructions. If we follow them, no one will be able to stand before us. To hear and trust one's own instincts is to live life dynamically. In censoring our thoughts know that God's direction always leads upward toward truth, righteousness, mercy, and love. Read Psalm 119:65–66.

PSALM 119
Verses 65–66

[65] Thou hast dwelt well with thy servant, O Lord, according to thy word.

[66] Teach me good judgment and knowledge: for I have believed thy commandments.

To Hear the Voice of God

*W*hen we hear the voice of God, it always prompts us to a sense of urgency. We realize that the greatest power in heaven and on earth has summoned us. God's voice is the voice of passion, and to hear it requires courage. It transcends human consciousness; it is spiritual and must be discerned spiritually. The voice of God always lets you know that God wants you to have life and have it more abundantly. Read Psalm 37:22–23.

PSALM 37
Verses 22–23

22 For such as be blessed of him shall inherit the earth; and they that be cursed of him shall be cut off.

23 The steps of a good man are ordered by the Lord: and he delighteth in his way.

Psalms for Aid in Spiritual Quest

WHEN SEARCHING FOR A TEACHER

Teachers, when they are also mentors, can help you make quantum leaps forward in your spiritual quest. However, since life is a constant cycle of change, a teacher who is appropriate at one stage may be inadequate at another. When searching for a teacher, search for one who has dedicated himself or herself to acquiring maximum awareness through God's Holy Spirit. The right teacher will help you explore in such a way that the end of your exploring will lead you to arrive at the point where you first began, yet know the place afresh, as for the first time. See Psalm 94:10 and Psalm 25:4–5.

PSALM 94
Verse 10

¹⁰ He that chastiseth the heathen, shall not he correct? He that teacheth man knowledge, shall he not know?

PSALM 25
Verses 4–5

⁴ Shew me thy ways, O Lord; teach me thy paths.

⁵ Lead me in thy truth, and teach me: for thou art the God of my salvation; on thee do I wait all the day.

STRENGTH FOR DEVELOPING
SPIRITUAL DISCIPLINE

Strength to develop spiritual discipline comes when you realize that you are God's; you are not a god. When you realize you belong to God, you learn to trust in God. Trust is essential because without it you have no basis for a relationship. Spiritual discipline helps us to develop an intimate relationship with God and to achieve victory over situations and individuals that would ordinarily cause us anxiety. Read all of Psalm 139 and memorize verses 23–24.

PSALM 139
Verses 23–24

23 Search me, O God, and know my heart: try me, and know my thoughts:

24 And see if there be any wicked way in me, and lead me in the way everlasting.

TO GAIN MORE TRUST IN GOD

*T*he Lord is a "shield and buckler" to them that trust in him. (Psalm 35:2) Reading God's words helps you develop an intimate relationship with God whereby God can trust you to do his work in the world. By reading scripture you learn from the experience of others that when God calls you for a certain task, you can know that it is God calling because it always *seems* beyond your capability. But if you step out in faith—long enough to attempt the impossible—God will send mighty forces to ensure success. Once you experience God working through you, your trust in God will increase as God learns that God can trust you. Read Psalm 37:3 and 5, and Psalm 3:5.

PSALM 37
Verses 3, 5

³ Trust in the Lord, and do good; so shalt thou dwell in the land, and verily thou shalt be fed.

⁵ Commit thy way unto the Lord; trust also in him; and he shall bring it to pass.

PSALM 3
Verse 5

⁵ I laid me down and slept; I awaked; for the Lord sustained me.

TO FIND UNQUESTIONING FAITH IN GOD'S EXISTENCE

*S*t. Augustine said it best years ago as he quoted scripture: "The fool hath said in his heart, There is no God." (Psalm 53:1) However, all of us will, like the prophet, ask from time to time, "How long O Lord? How long will thy hide thyself from me. Will thy hide thyself forever?" If ever you question the existence of God, read the thirty-eighth and thirty-ninth chapters of the book of Job. It will cause you to "Trust in the Lord with all thine heart; and lean not unto thine own understanding" (Proverbs 3:5). Then read Psalm 118, verse 8.

PSALM 118
Verse 8

⁸ It is better to trust in the Lord than to put confidence in man.

FOR A GREATER SENSE OF GOD'S PRESENCE

*T*o have a greater sense of God's presence, you must take time to center yourself in God. You must withdraw from the vaingloriousness of life and be still. Then draw near with a true heart in full assurance. If you draw near to God, God will draw near to you. When you do this, you will be able to bask in God's presence wherever you may go. Read Psalm 73, verse 28.

PSALM 73
Verse 28

28 But it is good for me to draw near to God: I have put my trust in the Lord God, that I may declare all thy works.

FOR GREATER INSIGHT INTO THE TRUE NATURE OF GOD

*S*cripture tells us that each person is made in the image of God. Like God we have been given dominion over the works of our hands. Similarly, we have the inspiration of the Almighty that gives us understanding. For a greater insight into the nature of God, spend many long hours searching the word of God, letting it become a part of your existence. Before you speak to anyone else in the morning pick up God's word and allow it to speak to you. Follow its teachings and you will gain greater insight into God as you become more like God. Read Psalm 8:1, 3–4.

PSALM 8
Verses 1, 3–4

[1] O Lord our Lord, how excellent is thy name in all the earth! who hast set thy glory above the heavens.

[3] When I consider thy heavens, the work of thy fingers, the moon and the stars, which thou hast ordained;

[4] What is man, that thou art mindful of him? and the son of man, that thou visitest him?

Psalms of Praise and Thanksgiving

FOR EDUCATION

Education is the knowledge, skill, and development gained through instruction and training. Because of the impact that education has in our society and the affect it has on individuals, it is glorified. When you realize that a good education is a gift from God, you will begin to cherish your knowledge—not for selfish gain, but to edify others. Joy and happiness come in the process of your sharing the knowledge you have with others. Thus, give praise and thanksgiving by reading Psalms 8, 19, 25, and 32. For brief reference read verses 1–10 and 14 of Psalm 19.

PSALM 19
Verses 1–10, 14

¹ The heavens declare the glory of God; and the firmament sheweth his handywork.

² Day unto day uttereth speech, and night unto night sheweth knowledge.

³ There is no speech nor language, where their voice is not heard.

⁴ Their line is gone out through all the earth, and their words to the end of the world. In them hath he set a tabernacle for the sun,

⁵ Which is as a bridegroom coming out of his chamber, and rejoiceth as a strong man to run a race.

⁶ His going forth is from the end of the heaven, and his circuit unto the ends of it: and there is nothing hid from the heat thereof.

⁷ The law of the Lord is perfect, converting the soul: the testimony of the Lord is sure, making wise the simple.

⁸ The statutes of the Lord are right, rejoicing the heart: the commandment of the Lord is pure, enlightening the eyes.

⁹ The fear of the Lord is clean, enduring for ever: the judgments of the Lord are true and righteous altogether.

¹⁰ More to be desired are they than gold, yea, than much fine gold: sweeter also than honey and the honeycomb.

¹⁴ Let the words of my mouth, and the meditation of my heart, be acceptable in thy sight, O Lord, my strength, and my redeemer.

FOR ONE'S CHILDHOOD

*Y*outh is a time of high energy and freedom. A childhood marked by innocence, love, joy, excitement, hard work, plenty of recreation and fun, parental discipline, and community support is a blessing from God. When we experience all these elements we are able to grow like a tender plant and flourish like an oak spreading its limbs. If, as a child, you were allowed to speak as a child, act as a child, and think like a child, when you became an adult, you were ready to put away childish things. Because of bad childhoods many adults grow older, but never actually grow up. If you were blessed with a good childhood, read psalms to offer praise and thanksgiving. Childhood shapes the person, as morning shapes the day. Psalm 45:15–17.

PSALM 45
Verses 15–17

15 With gladness and rejoicing shall they be brought: they shall enter into the king's palace.

16 Instead of thy fathers shall be thy children, whom thou mayest make princes in all the earth.

17 I will make thy name to be remembered in all generations: therefore shall the people praise thee for ever and ever.

FOR ONE'S HEALTH

*O*ne may accumulate material possessions in abundance and have status recognized by the world, but if the body or mind is racked with disease and void of vigor and vitality, there is little satisfaction and happiness is rare. Guarding your health should be a nonnegotiable priority. If you have health in mind, body, and spirit, there is much reason to offer prayers of gratitude to the creator. See Psalm 103:1–3.

PSALM 103
Verses 1–3

¹ Bless the Lord, O my soul: and all that is within me, bless his holy name.

² Bless the Lord, O my soul, and forget not all his benefits:

³ Who forgiveth all thine iniquities; who healeth all thy diseases;

FOR ONE'S FAMILY

*F*amily generally is a term used to refer to persons who are related by blood or relation. Blessed are you, however, if you are part of a community that is constantly growing as a family. In a community there are persons who have come to depend on one another. Loyalty, love, respect, common interests, and dependability usually make for a strong family. Favored are you if you are fortunate enough to be under such covering. Psalm 107: 40–42.

PSALM 107
Verses 40–42

[40] He poureth contempt upon princes, and causeth them to wander in the wilderness, where there is no way.

[41] Yet setteth he the poor on high from affliction, and maketh him families like a flock.

[42] The righteous shall see it, and rejoice: and all iniquity shall stop her mouth.

FOR ONE'S CHILDREN

*T*o have the purity of a child's hug or the profundity of a statement posed out of a child's raw truth is a blessing from God. In later life as parents grow weak, children grow strong. Blessed are aged parents who have children at their sides. Psalm 147: 11–13.

PSALM 147
Verses 11–13

11 The Lord taketh pleasure in them that fear him,
in those that hope in his mercy.

12 Praise the Lord, O Jerusalem; praise thy God,
O Zion.

13 For he hath strengthened the bars of thy gates;
he hath blessed thy children within thee.

FOR ONE'S PARENTS

*P*arents are to be honored and are to carry themselves in an honorable fashion. They should not provoke their children to wrath by being themselves disobedient to the tenants of God. (Ephesians 6:4) It is through the honoring of parents that God gives a promise of our days being long upon the land, which the Lord thy God giveth thee. (Ephesians 6:2, 3) Read Psalm 128.

PSALM 128
Verses 1–6

[1] Blessed is every one that feareth the Lord; that walketh in his ways.

[2] For thou shalt eat the labour of thine hands: happy shalt thou be, and it shall be well with thee.

[3] Thy wife shall be as a fruitful vine by the sides of thine house: thy children like olive plants round about thy table.

[4] Behold, that thus shall the man be blessed that feareth the Lord.

[5] The Lord shall bless thee out of Zion: and thou shalt see the good of Jerusalem all the days of thy life.

[6] Yea, thou shalt see thy children's children, and peace upon Israel.

FOR FRIENDS

*F*riends bear one another's burdens. They come together in times of need. They share moments of happiness. They share mutual affection and respect. They are able to agree and disagree and keep their relationship strong. Companionship coupled with friendship is a treasure. If you have true friends, offer thanks by reading. Psalm 35:14 and Psalm 108: 1–4.

PSALM 35
Verse 14

[14] I behaved myself as though he had been my friend or brother: I bowed down heavily, as one that mourneth for his mother.

PSALM 108
Verses 1–4

[1] O God, my heart is fixed; I will sing and give praise, even with my glory.

[2] Awake, psaltery and harp: I myself will awake early.

[3] I will praise thee, O Lord, among the people: and I will sing praises unto thee among the nations.

[4] For thy mercy is great above the heavens: and thy truth reacheth unto the clouds.

FOR ONE'S CHURCH

A church is more than the building, it is a community of believers. Whether it is a local body or an entire denomination, God must be the true head. When Christ is the head, all are invited to the banquet. If any are excluded, it is not a church but an organization operating under the church label. If you are part of a true church, this is reason to rejoice. Offer praise and thanksgiving by reading Psalm 32:1–2 and Psalm 33: 1–5.

PSALM 32
Verses 1–2

1 Blessed is he whose transgression is forgiven, whose sin is covered.

2 Blessed is the man unto whom the Lord imputeth not iniquity, and in whose spirit there is no guile.

PSALM 33
Verses 1–5

1 Rejoice in the Lord, O ye righteous: for praise is comely for the upright.

2 Praise the Lord with harp: sing unto him with the psaltery and an instrument of ten strings.

3 Sing unto him a new song; play skillfully with a loud noise.

4 For the word of the Lord is right; and all his works are done in truth.

5 He loveth righteousness and judgment: the earth is full of the goodness of the Lord.

FOR ONE'S WORK

*A*nything unused becomes unusable. Idleness can cause you to waste away. Thus it is a blessing to have work to perform. Commit your work unto the Lord, and do it as if unto God Almighty. Then you can be assured that your efforts will bring forth much fruit. Any work that is honest is honorable. To do one's best in whatever has been your lot pleases God. One who shows diligence and faithfulness when given a small task will be given more to do. Read Psalm 103:1–2.

PSALM 103
Verses 1–2

[1] Bless the Lord, O my soul: and all that is within me, bless his holy name.

[2] Bless the Lord, O my soul, and forget not all his benefits:

FOR ONE'S POSSESSIONS

*P*ossessions are temporal things. Yet they are not to be despised. They are to be appreciated and used to bring one comfort and joy. Where there are possessions rightfully gained, there is also the presence of the Lord. Do not put your trust in possessions, but always show appreciation for them. It's not what one acquires, but how one cares for one's possessions. Show God your appreciation, by caring for what has been given and by sharing with others. Read Psalm 44:1–3 and be reminded that your possessions are by God's favor.

PSALM 44
Verses 1–3

¹ We have heard with our ears, O God, our fathers have told us, what work thou didst in their days, in the times of old.

² How thou didst drive out the heathen with thy hand, and plantedst them; how thou didst afflict the people, and cast them out.

³ For they got not the land in possession by their own sword, neither did their own arm save them: but thy right hand, and thine arm, and the light of thy countenance, because thou hadst a favour unto them.

FOR GOD'S PRESENCE

*N*ever can we go from the presence of the Lord. To acknowledge God's abiding presence instantly brings blessings. If you acknowledge God in everything you do, the spirit of the Lord will be your guide. When you follow in the steps of Divine Guidance, your path will be lighted. We all desire a long life, but a full life comes only when we feel the indwelling of God's Holy Spirit. When you want to meditate on God's omnipresence and want to praise God for faithfully leading you through and around dangers seen and unseen, focus on verses 7 and 12–13 of Psalm 140; verses 1–6 of Psalm 13; verses 5–11 of Psalm 16; and verses 1–4 of Psalm 11.

PSALM 140
Verses 7, 12–13

7 O God the Lord, the strength of my salvation, thou hast covered my head in the day of battle.

12 I know that the Lord will maintain the cause of the afflicted, and the right of the poor.

13 Surely the righeous shall give thanks unto thy name: the upright shall dwell in thy presence.

PSALM 13
Verses 1–6

1 How long wilt thou forget me, O Lord? forever? how long wilt thou hide thy face from me?

2 How long shall I take counsel in my soul, having sorrow in my heart daily? how long shall mine enemy be exalted over me?

3 Consider and hear me, O Lord my God: lighten mine eyes, lest I sleep the sleep of death.

⁴ Lest mine enemy say, I have prevailed against him; and those that trouble me rejoice when I am moved.

⁵ But I have trusted in thy mercy; my heart shall rejoice in thy salvation.

⁶ I will sing unto the Lord, because he hath dealt bountifully with me.

PSALM 16
Verses 5–11

⁵ The Lord is the portion of mine inheritance and of my cup: thou maintainest my lot.

⁶ The lines are fallen unto me in pleasant places; yea, I have a goodly heritage.

⁷ I will bless the Lord, who hath given me counsel: my reins also instruct me in the night seasons.

⁸ I have set the Lord always before me: because he is at my right hand, I shall not be moved.

⁹ Therefore my heart is glad, and my glory rejoiceth: my flesh also shall rest in hope.

¹⁰ For thou wilt not leave my soul in hell; neither wilt thou suffer thine Holy One to see corruption.

¹¹ Thou wilt shew me the path of life: in thy presence is fulness of joy; at thy right hand there are pleasures for evermore.

PSALM 11
Verses 1–4

[1] In the Lord put I my trust: how say ye to my soul, Flee as a bird to your mountain?

[2] For, lo, the wicked bend their bow, they make ready their arrow upon the string, that they may privily shoot at the upright in heart.

[3] If the foundations be destroyed, what can the righteous do?

[4] The Lord is in his holy temple, the Lord's throne is in heaven: his eyes behold, his eyelids try, the children of men.

The Book of
Psalms

(King James Version)

Psalm 1

Blessed is the man that walketh not in the counsel of the ungodly, nor standeth in the way of sinners, nor sitteth in the seat of the scornful.

2 But his delight is in the law of the Lord; and in his law doth he meditate day and night.

3 And he shall be like a tree planted by the rivers of water, that bringeth forth his fruit in his season; his leaf also shall not wither; and whatsoever he doeth shall prosper.

4 The ungodly are not so: but are like the chaff which the wind driveth away.

5 Therefore the ungodly shall not stand in the judgment, nor sinners in the congregation of the righteous.

6 For the Lord knoweth the way of the righteous: but the way of the ungodly shall perish.

Psalm 2

Why do the heathen rage, and the people imagine a vain thing?

2 The kings of the earth set themselves, and the rulers take counsel together, against the Lord, and against his anointed, saying,

3 Let us break their bands asunder, and cast away their cords from us.

4 He that sitteth in the heavens shall laugh: the Lord shall have them in derision.

5 Then shall he speak unto them in his wrath, and vex them in his sore displeasure.

⁶ Yet have I set my king upon my holy hill of Zion.

⁷ I will declare the decree: the Lord hath said unto me, Thou art my Son; this day have I begotten thee.

⁸ Ask of me, and I shall give thee the heathen for thine inheritance, and the uttermost parts of the earth for thy possession.

⁹ Thou shalt break them with a rod of iron; thou shalt dash them in pieces like a potter's vessel.

¹⁰ Be wise now therefore, O ye kings: be instructed, ye judges of the earth.

¹¹ Serve the Lord with fear, and rejoice with trembling.

¹² Kiss the Son, lest he be angry, and ye perish from the way, when his wrath is kindled but a little. Blessed are all they that put their trust in him.

Psalm 3

Lord, how are they increased that trouble me! many are they that rise up against me.

² Many there be which say of my soul, There is no help for him in God. Selah.

³ But thou, O Lord, art a shield for me; my glory, and the lifter up of mine head.

⁴ I cried unto the Lord with my voice, and he heard me out of his holy hill. Selah.

⁵ I laid me down and slept; I awaked; for the Lord sustained me.

⁶ I will not be afraid of ten thousands of people, that have set themselves against me round about.

⁷ Arise, O Lord; save me, O my God: for thou hast smitten all mine enemies upon the cheek bone; thou hast broken the teeth of the ungodly.

[8] Salvation belongeth unto the Lord: thy blessing is upon thy people. Selah.

Psalm 4

Hear me when I call, O God of my righteousness: thou hast enlarged me when I was in distress; have mercy upon me, and hear my prayer.

[2] O ye sons of men, how long will ye turn my glory into shame? how long will ye love vanity, and seek after leasing? Selah.

[3] But know that the Lord hath set apart him that is godly for himself: the Lord will hear when I call unto him.

[4] Stand in awe, and sin not: commune with your own heart upon your bed, and be still. Selah.

[5] Offer the sacrifices of righteousness, and put your trust in the Lord.

[6] There be many that say, Who will shew us any good? Lord, lift thou up the light of thy countenance upon us.

[7] Thou hast put gladness in my heart, more than in the time that their corn and their wine increased.

[8] I will both lay me down in peace, and sleep: for thou, Lord, only makest me dwell in safety.

Psalm 5

Give ear to my words, O Lord, consider my meditation.

[2] Hearken unto the voice of my cry, my King, and my God: for unto thee will I pray.

[3] My voice shalt thou hear in the morning, O Lord; in the morning will I direct my prayer unto thee, and will look up.

[4] For thou art not a God that hath pleasure in wickedness: neither shall evil dwell with thee.

⁵ The foolish shall not stand in thy sight: thou hatest all workers of iniquity.

⁶ Thou shalt destroy them that speak leasing: the Lord will abhor the bloody and deceitful man.

⁷ But as for me, I will come into thy house in the multitude of thy mercy: and in thy fear will I worship toward thy holy temple.

⁸ Lead me, O Lord, in thy righteousness because of mine enemies; make thy way straight before my face.

⁹ For there is no faithfulness in their mouth; their inward part is very wickedness; their throat is an open sepulchre; they flatter with their tongue.

¹⁰ Destroy thou them, O God; let them fall by their own counsels; cast them out in the multitude of their transgressions; for they have rebelled against thee.

¹¹ But let all those that put their trust in thee rejoice: let them ever shout for joy, because thou defendest them: let them also that love thy name be joyful in thee.

¹² For thou, Lord, wilt bless the righteous; with favour wilt thou compass him as with a shield.

Psalm 6

O Lord, rebuke me not in thine anger, neither chasten me in thy hot displeasure.

² Have mercy upon me, O Lord; for I am weak: O Lord, heal me; for my bones are vexed.

³ My soul is also sore vexed: but thou, O Lord, how long?

⁴ Return, O Lord, deliver my soul: oh save me for thy mercies' sake.

⁵ For in death there is no remembrance of thee: in the grave who shall give thee thanks?

⁶ I am weary with my groaning; all the night make I my bed to swim; I water my couch with my tears.

⁷ Mine eye is consumed because of grief; it waxeth old because of all mine enemies.

⁸ Depart from me, all ye workers of iniquity; for the Lord hath heard the voice of my weeping.

⁹ The Lord hath heard my supplication; the Lord will receive my prayer.

¹⁰ Let all mine enemies be ashamed and sore vexed: let them return and be ashamed suddenly.

Psalm 7

O Lord my God, in thee do I put my trust: save me from all them that persecute me, and deliver me:

² Lest he tear my soul like a lion, rending it in pieces, while there is none to deliver.

³ O Lord my God, if I have done this; if there be iniquity in my hands;

⁴ If I have rewarded evil unto him that was at peace with me; (yea, I have delivered him that without cause is mine enemy:)

⁵ Let the enemy persecute my soul, and take it; yea, let them tread down my life upon the earth, and lay mine honour in the dust. Selah.

⁶ Arise, O Lord, in thine anger, lift up thyself because of the rage of mine enemies: and awake for me to the judgment that thou hast commanded.

⁷ So shall the congregation of the people compass thee about: for their sakes therefore return thou on high.

⁸ The Lord shall judge the people: judge me, O Lord, according to my righteousness, and according to mine integrity that is in me.

⁹ Oh let the wickedness of the wicked come to an end; but establish the just; for the righteous God trieth the hearts and reins.

¹⁰ My defense is of God, which saveth the upright in heart.

¹¹ God judgeth the righteous, and God is angry with the wicked every day.

¹² If he turn not, he will whet his sword; he hath bent his bow, and made it ready.

¹³ He hath also prepared for him the instruments of death; he ordaineth his arrows against the persecutors.

¹⁴ Behold, he travaileth with iniquity, and hath conceived mischief, and brought forth falsehood.

¹⁵ He made a pit, and digged it, and is fallen into the ditch which he made.

¹⁶ His mischief shall return upon his own head, and his violent dealing shall come down upon his own pate.

¹⁷ I will praise the Lord according to his righteousness: and will sing praise to the name of the Lord most high.

Psalm 8

O Lord our Lord, how excellent is thy name in all the earth! who hast set thy glory above the heavens.

² Out of the mouth of babes and sucklings hast thou ordained strength because of thine enemies, that thou mightest still the enemy and the avenger.

³ When I consider thy heavens, the work of thy fingers, the moon and the stars, which thou hast ordained;

⁴ What is man, that thou art mindful of him? and the son of man, that thou visitest him?

⁵ For thou hast made him a little lower than the angels, and hast crowned him with glory and honour.

⁶ Thou madest him to have dominion over the works of thy hands; thou hast put all things under his feet:

⁷ All sheep and oxen, yea, and the beasts of the field;

⁸ The fowl of the air, and the fish of the sea, and whatsoever passeth through the paths of the seas.

⁹ O Lord our Lord, how excellent is thy name in all the earth!

Psalm 9

I will praise thee, O Lord, with my whole heart; I will shew forth all thy marvellous works.

² I will be glad and rejoice in thee: I will sing praise to thy name, O thou most High.

³ When mine enemies are turned back, they shall fall and perish at thy presence.

⁴ For thou has maintained my right and my cause; thou sattest in the throne judging right.

⁵ Thou hast rebuked the heathen, thou hast destroyed the wicked, thou hast put out their name for ever and ever.

⁶ O thou enemy, destructions are come to a perpetual end: and thou hast destroyed cities; their memorial is perished with them.

⁷ But the Lord shall endure forever: he hath prepared his throne for judgment.

⁸ And he shall judge the world in righteousness, he shall minister judgment to the people in uprightness.

⁹ The Lord also will be a refuge for the oppressed, a refuge in times of trouble.

¹⁰ And they that know thy name will put their trust in thee: for thou, Lord, hast not forsaken them that seek thee.

¹¹ Sing praises to the Lord, which dwelleth in Zion: declare among the people his doings.

¹² When he maketh inquisition for blood, he remembereth them: he forgetteth not the cry of the humble.

¹³ Have mercy upon me, O Lord; consider my trouble which I suffer of them that hate me, thou that liftest me up from the gates of death:

¹⁴ That I may shew forth all thy praise in the gates of the daughter of Zion: I will rejoice in thy salvation.

¹⁵ The heathen are sunk down in the pit that they made: in the net which they hid is their own foot taken.

¹⁶ The Lord is known by the judgment which he executeth: the wicked is snared in the work of his own hands. Higgaion. Selah.

¹⁷ The wicked shall be turned into hell, and all the nations that forget God.

¹⁸ For the needy shall not alway be forgotten: the expectation of the poor shall not perish for ever.

¹⁹ Arise, O Lord; let not man prevail: let the heathen be judged in thy sight.

²⁰ Put them in fear, O Lord: that the nations may know themselves to be but men. Selah.

Psalm 10

Why standest thou afar off, O Lord? why hidest thou thyself in times of trouble?

² The wicked in his pride doth persecute the poor: let them be taken in the devices that they have imagined.

³ For the wicked boasteth of his heart's desire, and blesseth the covetous, whom the Lord abhorreth.

⁴ The wicked, through the pride of his countenance, will not seek after God: God is not in all his thoughts.

⁵ His ways are always grievous; thy judgments are far above out of his sight: as for all his enemies, he puffeth at them.

⁶ He hath said in his heart, I shall not be moved: for I shall never be in adversity.

⁷ His mouth is full of cursing and deceit and fraud: under his tongue is mischief and vanity.

⁸ He sitteth in the lurking places of the villages: in the secret places doth he murder the innocent: his eyes are privily set against the poor.

⁹ He lieth in wait secretly as a lion in his den: he lieth in wait to catch the poor: he doth catch the poor, when he draweth him into his net.

¹⁰ He croucheth, and humbleth himself, that the poor may fall by his strong ones.

¹¹ He hath said in his heart, God hath forgotten: he hideth his face; he will never see it.

¹² Arise, O Lord; O God, lift up thine hand: forget not the humble.

¹³ Wherefore doth the wicked contemn God? he hath said in his heart, Thou wilt not require it.

¹⁴ Thou hast seen it; for thou beholdest mischief and spite, to requite it with thy hand: the poor committeth himself unto thee; thou art the helper of the fatherless.

¹⁵ Break thou the arm of the wicked and the evil man: seek out his wickedness till thou find none.

¹⁶ The Lord is King for ever and ever: the heathen are perished out of his land.

[17] Lord, thou hast heard the desire of the humble: thou wilt prepare their heart, thou wilt cause thine ear to hear:

[18] To judge the fatherless and the oppressed, that the man of the earth may no more oppress.

Psalm 11

In the Lord put I my trust: how say ye to my soul, Flee as a bird to your mountain?

[2] For, lo, the wicked bend their bow, they make ready their arrow upon the string, that they may privily shoot at the upright in heart.

[3] If the foundations be destroyed, what can the righteous do?

[4] The Lord is in his holy temple, the Lord's throne is in heaven: his eyes behold, his eyelids try, the children of men.

[5] The Lord trieth the righteous: but the wicked and him that loveth violence his soul hateth.

[6] Upon the wicked he shall rain snares, fire and brimstone, and an horrible tempest: this shall be the portion of their cup.

[7] For the righteous Lord loveth righteousness; his countenance doth behold the upright.

Psalm 12

Help, Lord; for the godly man ceaseth; for the faithful fail from among the children of men.

[2] They speak vanity every one with his neighbour: with flattering lips and with a double heart do they speak.

[3] The Lord shall cut off all flattering lips, and the tongue that speaketh proud things:

[4] Who have said, With our tongue will we prevail; our lips are our own: who is lord over us?

⁵ For the oppression of the poor, for the sighing of the needy, now will I arise, saith the Lord; I will set him in safety from him that puffeth at him.

⁶ The words of the Lord are pure words: as silver tried in a furnace of earth, purified seven times.

⁷ Thou shalt keep them, O Lord, thou shalt preserve them from this generation for ever.

⁸ The wicked walk on every side, when the vilest men are exalted.

Psalm 13

How long wilt thou forget me, O Lord? for ever? how long wilt thou hide thy face from me?

² How long shall I take counsel in my soul, having sorrow in my heart daily? how long shall mine enemy be exalted over me?

³ Consider and hear me, O Lord my God: lighten mine eyes, lest I sleep the sleep of death.

⁴ Lest mine enemy say, I have prevailed against him; and those that trouble me rejoice when I am moved.

⁵ But I have trusted in thy mercy; my heart shall rejoice in thy salvation.

⁶ I will sing unto the Lord, because he hath dealt bountifully with me.

Psalm 14

The fool hath said in his heart, There is no God. They are corrupt, they have done abominable works, there is none that doeth good.

² The Lord looked down from heaven upon the children of men, to see if there were any that did understand, and seek God.

³ They are all gone aside, they are all together become filthy: there is none that doeth good, no, not one.

⁴ Have all the workers of iniquity no knowledge? who eat up my people as they eat bread, and call not upon the Lord.

⁵ There were they in great fear: for God is in the generation of the righteous.

⁶ Ye have shamed the counsel of the poor, because the Lord is his refuge.

⁷ Oh that the salvation of Israel were come out of Zion! when the Lord bringeth back the captivity of his people, Jacob shall rejoice, and Israel shall be glad.

Psalm 15

Lord, who shall abide in thy tabernacle? who shall dwell in thy holy hill?

² He that walketh uprightly, and worketh righteousness, and speaketh the truth in his heart.

³ He that backbiteth not with his tongue, nor doeth evil to his neighbour, nor taketh up a reproach against his neighbour.

⁴ In whose eyes a vile person is contemned; but he honoureth them that fear the Lord. He that sweareth to his own hurt, and changeth not.

⁵ He that putteth not out his money to usury, nor taketh reward against the innocent. He that doeth these things shall never be moved.

Psalm 16

Preserve me, O God: for in thee do I put my trust.

² O my soul, thou hast said unto the Lord, Thou art my Lord: my goodness extendeth not to thee;

³ But to the saints that are in the earth, and to the excellent, in whom is all my delight.

⁴ Their sorrows shall be multiplied that hasten after another god: their drink offerings of blood will I not offer, nor take up their names into my lips.

⁵ The Lord is the portion of mine inheritance and of my cup: thou maintainest my lot.

⁶ The lines are fallen unto me in pleasant places; yea, I have a goodly heritage.

⁷ I will bless the Lord, who hath given me counsel: my reins also instruct me in the night seasons.

⁸ I have set the Lord always before me: because he is at my right hand, I shall not be moved.

⁹ Therefore my heart is glad, and my glory rejoiceth: my flesh also shall rest in hope.

¹⁰ For thou wilt not leave my soul in hell; neither wilt thou suffer thine Holy One to see corruption.

¹¹ Thou wilt shew me the path of life: in thy presence is fulness of joy; at thy right hand there are pleasures for evermore.

Psalm 17

Hear the right, O Lord, attend unto my cry, give ear unto my prayer, that goeth not out of feigned lips.

² Let my sentence come forth from thy presence; let thine eyes behold the things that are equal.

³ Thou has proved mine heart; thou hast visited me in the night; thou hast tried me, and shalt find nothing; I am purposed that my mouth shall not transgress.

⁴ Concerning the words of men, by the word of thy lips I have kept me from the paths of the destroyer.

⁵ Hold up my goings in thy paths, that my footsteps slip not.

⁶ I have called upon thee, for thou wilt hear me, O God: incline thine ear unto me, and hear my speech.

⁷ Shew thy marvellous lovingkindness, O thou that savest by thy right hand them which put their trust in thee from those that rise up against them.

⁸ Keep me as the apple of the eye, hide me under the shadow of thy wings,

⁹ From the wicked that oppress me, from my deadly enemies, who compass me about.

¹⁰ They are inclosed in their own fat: with their mouth they speak proudly.

¹¹ They have now compassed us in our steps: they have set their eyes bowing down to the earth;

¹² Like as a lion that is greedy of his prey, and as it were a young lion lurking in secret places.

¹³ Arise, O Lord, disappoint him, cast him down: deliver my soul from the wicked, which is thy sword:

¹⁴ From men which are thy hand, O Lord, from men of the world, which have their portion in this life, and whose belly thou fillest with thy hid treasure: they are full of children, and leave the rest of their substance to their babes.

¹⁵ As for me, I will behold thy face in righteousness: I shall be satisfied, when I awake, with thy likeness.

Psalm 18

I will love thee, O Lord, my strength.

² The Lord is my rock, and my fortress, and my deliverer; my God, my strength, in whom I will trust; my buckler, and the horn of my salvation, and my high tower.

[3] I will call upon the Lord, who is worthy to be praised: so shall I be saved from mine enemies.

[4] The sorrows of death compassed me, and the floods of ungodly men made me afraid.

[5] The sorrows of hell compassed me about: the snares of death prevented me.

[6] In my distress I called upon the Lord, and cried unto my God: he heard my voice out of his temple, and my cry came before him, even into his ears.

[7] Then the earth shook and trembled; the foundations also of the hills moved and were shaken, because he was wroth.

[8] There went up a smoke out of his nostrils, and fire out of his mouth devoured: coals were kindled by it.

[9] He bowed the heavens also, and came down: and darkness was under his feet.

[10] And he rode upon a cherub, and did fly: yea, he did fly upon the wings of the wind.

[11] He made darkness his secret place; his pavilion round about him were dark waters and thick clouds of the skies.

[12] At the brightness that was before him his thick clouds passed, hail stones and coals of fire.

[13] The Lord also thundered in the heavens, and the Highest gave his voice; hail stones and coals of fire.

[14] Yea, he sent out his arrows, and scattered them; and he shot out lightnings, and discomfited them.

[15] Then the channels of waters were seen, and the foundations of the world were discovered at thy rebuke, O Lord, at the blast of the breath of thy nostrils.

[16] He sent from above, he took me, he drew me out of many waters.

[17] He delivered me from my strong enemy, and from them which hated me: for they were too strong for me.

[18] They prevented me in the day of my calamity: but the Lord was my stay.

[19] He brought me forth also into a large place; he delivered me, because he delighted in me.

[20] The Lord rewarded me according to my righteousness; according to the cleanness of my hands hath he recompensed me.

[21] For I have kept the ways of the Lord, and have not wickedly departed from my God.

[22] For all his judgments were before me, and I did not put away his statutes from me.

[23] I was also upright before him, and I kept myself from mine iniquity.

[24] Therefore hath the Lord recompensed me according to my righteousness, according to the cleanness of my hands in his eyesight.

[25] With the merciful thou wilt shew thyself merciful; with an upright man thou wilt shew thyself upright;

[26] With the pure thou wilt shew thyself pure; and with the froward thou wilt shew thyself froward.

[27] For thou wilt save the afflicted people; but wilt bring down high looks.

[28] For thou wilt light my candle: the Lord my God will enlighten my darkness.

[29] For by thee I have run through a troop; and by my God have I leaped over a wall.

[30] As for God, his way is perfect: the word of the Lord is tried: he is a buckler to all those that trust in him.

[31] For who is God save the Lord? or who is a rock save our God?

[32] It is God that girdeth me with strength, and maketh my way perfect.

[33] He maketh my feet like hinds' feet, and setteth me upon my high places.

[34] He teacheth my hands to war, so that a bow of steel is broken by mine arms.

[35] Thou hast also given me the shield of thy salvation: and thy right hand hath holden me up, and thy gentleness hath made me great.

[36] Thou hast enlarged my steps under me, that my feet did not slip.

[37] I have pursued mine enemies, and overtaken them: neither did I turn again till they were consumed.

[38] I have wounded them that they were not able to rise: they are fallen under my feet.

[39] For thou hast girded me with strength unto the battle: thou hast subdued under me those that rose up against me.

[40] Thou hast also given me the necks of mine enemies; that I might destroy them that hate me.

[41] They cried, but there was none to save them: even unto the Lord, but he answered them not.

[42] Then did I beat them small as the dust before the wind: I did cast them out as the dirt in the streets.

[43] Thou hast delivered me from the strivings of the people; and thou hast made me the head of the heathen: a people whom I have not known shall serve me.

[44] As soon as they hear of me, they shall obey me: the strangers shall submit themselves unto me.

[45] The strangers shall fade away, and be afraid out of their close places.

⁴⁶ The Lord liveth; and blessed be my rock; and let the God of my salvation be exalted.

⁴⁷ It is God that avengeth me, and subdueth the people under me.

⁴⁸ He delivereth me from mine enemies: yea, thou liftest me up above those that rise up against me: thou hast delivered me from the violent man.

⁴⁹ Therefore will I give thanks unto thee, O Lord, among the heathen, and sing praises unto thy name.

⁵⁰ Great deliverance giveth he to his king; and sheweth mercy to his anointed, to David, and to his seed for evermore.

Psalm 19

The heavens declare the glory of God; and the firmament sheweth his handywork.

² Day unto day uttereth speech, and night unto night sheweth knowledge.

³ There is no speech nor language, where their voice is not heard.

⁴ Their line is gone out through all the earth, and their words to the end of the world. In them hath he set a tabernacle for the sun,

⁵ Which is as a bridegroom coming out of his chamber, and rejoiceth as a strong man to run a race.

⁶ His going forth is from the end of the heaven, and his circuit unto the ends of it: and there is nothing hid from the heat thereof.

⁷ The law of the Lord is perfect, converting the soul: the testimony of the Lord is sure, making wise the simple.

⁸ The statutes of the Lord are right, rejoicing the heart: the commandment of the Lord is pure, enlightening the eyes.

⁹ The fear of the Lord is clean, enduring for ever: the judgments of the Lord are true and righteous altogether.

¹⁰ More to be desired are they than gold, yea, than much fine gold: sweeter also than honey and the honeycomb.

¹¹ Moreover by them is thy servant warned: and in keeping of them there is great reward.

¹² Who can understand his errors? cleanse thou me from secret faults.

¹³ Keep back thy servant also from presumptuous sins; let them not have dominion over me: then shall I be upright, and I shall be innocent from the great transgression.

¹⁴ Let the words of my mouth, and the meditation of my heart, be acceptable in thy sight, O Lord, my strength, and my redeemer.

Psalm 20

The Lord hear thee in the day of trouble; the name of the God of Jacob defend thee;

² Send thee help from the sanctuary, and strengthen thee out of Zion;

³ Remember all thy offerings, and accept thy burnt sacrifice; Selah.

⁴ Grant thee according to thine own heart, and fulfil all thy counsel.

⁵ We will rejoice in thy salvation, and in the name of our God we will set up our banners: the Lord fulfil all thy petitions.

⁶ Now know I that the Lord saveth his anointed; he will hear him from his holy heaven with the saving strength of his right hand,

⁷ Some trust in chariots, and some in horses: but we will remember the name of the Lord our God.

⁸ They are brought down and fallen: but we are risen, and stand upright.

⁹ Save, Lord: let the king hear us when we call.

Psalm 21

The king shall joy in thy strength, O Lord; and in thy salvation how greatly shall he rejoice!

[2] Thou hast given him his heart's desire, and hast not withholden the request of his lips. Selah.

[3] For thou preventest him with the blessings of goodness: thou settest a crown of pure gold on his head.

[4] He asked life of thee, and thou gavest it him, even length of days for ever and ever.

[5] His glory is great in thy salvation: honour and majesty hast thou laid upon him.

[6] For thou hast made him most blessed for ever: thou hast made him exceeding glad with thy countenance.

[7] For the king trusteth in the Lord, and through the mercy of the most High he shall not be moved.

[8] Thine hand shall find out all thine enemies: thy right hand shall find out those that hate thee.

[9] Thou shalt make them as a fiery oven in the time of thine anger: the Lord shall swallow them up in his wrath, and the fire shall devour them.

[10] Their fruit shalt thou destroy from the earth, and their seed from among the children of men.

[11] For they intended evil against thee: they imagined a mischievous device, which they are not able to perform.

[12] Therefore shalt thou make them turn their back, when thou shalt make ready thine arrows upon thy strings against the face of them.

[13] Be thou exalted, Lord, in thine own strength: so will we sing and praise thy power.

Psalm 22

My God, my God, why hast thou forsaken me? why art thou so far from helping me, and from the words of my roaring?

2 O my God, I cry in the daytime, but thou hearest not; and in the night season, and am not silent.

3 But thou art holy, O thou that inhabitest the praises of Israel.

4 Our fathers trusted in thee: they trusted, and thou didst deliver them.

5 They cried unto thee, and were delivered: they trusted in thee, and were not confounded.

6 But I am a worm, and no man; a reproach of men, and despised of the people.

7 All they that see me laugh me to scorn: they shoot out the lip, they shake the head, saying,

8 He trusted on the Lord that he would deliver him: let him deliver him, seeing he delighted in him.

9 But thou art he that took me out of the womb: thou didst make me hope when I was upon my mother's breasts.

10 I was cast upon thee from the womb: thou art my God from my mother's belly.

11 Be not far from me; for trouble is near; for there is none to help.

12 Many bulls have compassed me: strong bulls of Bashan have beset me round.

13 They gaped upon me with their mouths, as a ravening and a roaring lion.

14 I am poured out like water, and all my bones are out of joint: my heart is like wax; it is melted in the midst of my bowels.

15 My strength is dried up like a potsherd; and my tongue cleaveth to my jaws; and thou hast brought me into the dust of death.

¹⁶ For dogs have compassed me: the assembly of the wicked have inciosed me: they pierced my hands and my feet.

¹⁷ I may tell all my bones: they look and stare upon me.

¹⁸ They part my garments among them, and cast lots upon my vesture.

¹⁹ But be not thou far from me, O Lord: O my strength, haste thee to help me.

²⁰ Deliver my soul from the sword; my darling from the power of the dog.

²¹ Save me from the lion's mouth: for thou hast heard me from the horns of the unicorns.

²² I will declare thy name unto my brethren: in the midst of the congregation will I praise thee.

²³ Ye that fear the Lord, praise him; all ye the seed of Jacob, glorify him; and fear him, all ye the seed of Israel.

²⁴ For he hath not despised nor abhorred the affliction of the afflicted; neither hath he hid his face from him; but when he cried unto him, he heard.

²⁵ My praise shall be of thee in the great congregation: I will pay my vows before them that fear him.

²⁶ The meek shall eat and be satisfied: they shall praise the Lord that seek him: your heart shall live for ever.

²⁷ All the ends of the world shall remember and turn unto the Lord: and all the kindreds of the nations shall worship before thee.

²⁸ For the kingdom is the Lord's: and he is the governor among the nations.

²⁹ All they that be fat upon earth shall eat and worship: all they that go down to the dust shall bow before him: and none can keep alive his own soul.

³⁰ A seed shall serve him; it shall be accounted to the Lord for a generation.

³¹ They shall come, and shall declare his righteousness unto a people that shall be born, that he hath done this.

Psalm 23

The Lord is my shepherd; I shall not want.

² He maketh me to lie down in green pastures: he leadeth me beside the still waters.

³ He restoreth my soul: he leadeth me in the paths of righteousness for his name's sake.

⁴ Yea, though I walk through the valley of the shadow of death, I will fear no evil: for thou art with me; thy rod and thy staff they comfort me.

⁵ Thou preparest a table before me in the presence of mine enemies: thou anointest my head with oil; my cup runneth over.

⁶ Surely goodness and mercy shall follow me all the days of my life: and I will dwell in the house of the Lord for ever.

Psalm 24

The earth is the Lord's, and the fulness thereof; the world, and they that dwell therein.

² For he hath founded it upon the seas, and established it upon the floods.

³ Who shall ascend into the hill of the Lord? or who shall stand in his holy place?

⁴ He that hath clean hands, and a pure heart; who hath not lifted up his soul unto vanity, nor sworn deceitfully.

⁵ He shall receive the blessing from the Lord, and righteousness from the God of his salvation.

⁶ This is the generation of them that seek him, that seek thy face, O Jacob. Selah.

⁷ Lift up your heads, O ye gates; and be ye lift up, ye everlasting doors; and the King of glory shall come in.

⁸ Who is this King of glory? The Lord strong and mighty, the Lord mighty in battle.

⁹ Lift up your heads, O ye gates; even lift them up, ye everlasting doors; and the King of glory shall come in.

¹⁰ Who is this King of glory? The Lord of hosts, he is the King of glory. Selah.

Psalm 25

Unto thee, O Lord, do I lift up my soul.

² O my God, I trust in thee: let me not be ashamed, let not mine enemies triumph over me.

³ Yea, let none that wait on thee be ashamed: let them be ashamed which transgress without cause.

⁴ Shew me thy ways, O Lord; teach me thy paths.

⁵ Lead me in thy truth, and teach me: for thou art the God of my salvation; on thee do I wait all the day.

⁶ Remember, O Lord, thy tender mercies and thy lovingkindnesses; for they have been ever of old.

⁷ Remember not the sins of my youth, nor my transgressions: according to thy mercy remember thou me for thy goodness' sake, O Lord.

⁸ Good and upright is the Lord: therefore will he teach sinners in the way.

⁹ The meek will he guide in judgment: and the meek will he teach his way.

[10] All the paths of the Lord are mercy and truth unto such as keep his covenant and his testimonies.

[11] For thy name's sake, O Lord, pardon mine iniquity; for it is great.

[12] What man is he that feareth the Lord? him shall he teach in the way that he shall choose.

[13] His soul shall dwell at ease; and his seed shall inherit the earth.

[14] The secret of the Lord is with them that fear him; and he will shew them his covenant.

[15] Mine eyes are ever toward the Lord; for he shall pluck my feet out of the net.

[16] Turn thee unto me, and have mercy upon me; for I am desolate and afflicted.

[17] The troubles of my heart are enlarged: O bring thou me out of my distresses.

[18] Look upon mine affliction and my pain; and forgive all my sins.

[19] Consider mine enemies; for they are many; and they hate me with cruel hatred.

[20] O keep my soul, and deliver me: let me not be ashamed; for I put my trust in thee.

[21] Let integrity and uprightness preserve me; for I wait on thee.

[22] Redeem Israel, O God, out of all his troubles.

Psalm 26

Judge me, O Lord; for I have walked in mine integrity: I have trusted also in the Lord; therefore I shall not slide.

[2] Examine me, O Lord, and prove me; try my reins and my heart.

[3] For thy lovingkindness is before mine eyes: and I have walked in thy truth.

⁴ I have not sat with vain persons, neither will I go in with dissemblers.

⁵ I have hated the congregation of evil doers; and will not sit with the wicked.

⁶ I will wash mine hands in innocency: so will I compass thine altar, O Lord.

⁷ That I may publish with the voice of thanksgiving, and tell of all thy wondrous works.

⁸ Lord, I have loved the habitation of thy house, and the place where thine honour dwelleth.

⁹ Gather not my soul with sinners, nor my life with bloody men:

¹⁰ In whose hands is mischief, and their right hand is full of bribes.

¹¹ But as for me, I will walk in mine integrity: redeem me, and be merciful unto me.

¹² My foot standeth in an even place: in the congregations will I bless the Lord.

Psalm 27

The Lord is my light and my salvation; whom shall I fear? the Lord is the strength of my life; of whom shall I be afraid?

² When the wicked, even mine enemies and my foes, came upon me to eat up my flesh, they stumbled and fell.

³ Though an host should encamp against me, my heart shall not fear: though war should rise against me, in this will I be confident.

⁴ One thing have I desired of the Lord, that will I seek after; that I may dwell in the house of the Lord all the days of my life, to behold the beauty of the Lord, and to inquire in his temple.

⁵ For in the time of trouble he shall hide me in his pavilion: in the secret of his tabernacle shall he hide me; he shall set me up upon a rock.

⁶ And now shall mine head be lifted up above mine enemies round about me: therefore will I offer in his tabernacle sacrifices of joy; I will sing, yea, I will sing praises unto the Lord.

⁷ Hear, O Lord, when I cry with my voice: have mercy also upon me, and answer me.

⁸ When thou saidst, Seek ye my face; my heart said unto thee, Thy face, Lord, will I seek.

⁹ Hide not thy face far from me; put not thy servant away in anger: thou hast been my help; leave me not, neither forsake me, O God of my salvation.

¹⁰ When my father and my mother forsake me, then the Lord will take me up.

¹¹ Teach me thy way, O Lord, and lead me in a plain path, because of mine enemies.

¹² Deliver me not over unto the will of mine enemies: for false witnesses are risen up against me, and such as breathe out cruelty.

¹³ I had fainted, unless I had believed to see the goodness of the Lord in the land of the living.

¹⁴ Wait on the Lord: be of good courage, and he shall strengthen thine heart: wait, I say, on the Lord.

Psalm 28

Unto thee will I cry, O Lord my rock; be not silent to me: lest, if thou be silent to me, I become like them that go down into the pit.

² Hear the voice of my supplications, when I cry unto thee, when I lift up my hands toward thy holy oracle.

³ Draw me not away with the wicked, and with the workers of iniquity, which speak peace to their neighbours, but mischief is in their hearts.

⁴ Give them according to their deeds, and according to the wickedness of their endeavours: give them after the work of their hands; render to them their desert.

⁵ Because they regard not the works of the Lord, nor the operation of his hands, he shall destroy them, and not build them up.

⁶ Blessed be the Lord, because he hath heard the voice of my supplications.

⁷ The Lord is my strength and my shield; my heart trusted in him, and I am helped: therefore my heart greatly rejoiceth; and with my song will I praise him.

⁸ The Lord is their strength, and he is the saving strength of his anointed.

⁹ Save thy people, and bless thine inheritance: feed them also, and lift them up for ever.

Psalm 29

Give unto the Lord, O ye mighty, give unto the Lord glory and strength.

² Give unto the Lord the glory due unto his name; worship the Lord in the beauty of holiness.

³ The voice of the Lord is upon the waters: the God of glory thundereth: the Lord is upon many waters.

⁴ The voice of the Lord is powerful; the voice of the Lord is full of majesty.

⁵ The voice of the Lord breaketh the cedars; yea, the Lord breaketh the cedars of Lebanon.

⁶ He maketh them also to skip like a calf; Lebanon and Sirion like a young unicorn.

⁷ The voice of the Lord divideth the flames of fire.

⁸ The voice of the Lord shaketh the wilderness; the Lord shaketh the wilderness of Kadesh.

⁹ The voice of the Lord maketh the hinds to calve, and discovereth the forests: and in his temple doth every one speak of his glory.

¹⁰ The Lord sitteth upon the flood; yea, the Lord sitteth King for ever.

¹¹ The Lord will give strength unto his people; the Lord will bless his people with peace.

Psalm 30

I will extol thee, O Lord; for thou hast lifted me up, and hast not made my foes to rejoice over me.

² O Lord my God, I cried unto thee, and thou hast healed me.

³ O Lord, thou hast brought up my soul from the grave: thou hast kept me alive, that I should not go down to the pit.

⁴ Sing unto the Lord, O ye saints of his, and give thanks at the remembrance of his holiness.

⁵ For his anger endureth but a moment; in his favour is life: weeping may endure for a night, but joy cometh in the morning.

⁶ And in my prosperity I said, I shall never be moved.

⁷ Lord, by thy favour thou hast made my mountain to stand strong: thou didst hide thy face, and I was troubled.

⁸ I cried to thee, O Lord; and unto the Lord I made supplication.

⁹ What profit is there in my blood, when I go down to the pit? Shall the dust praise thee? shall it declare thy truth?

¹⁰ Hear, O Lord, and have mercy upon me: Lord, be thou my helper.

¹¹ Thou hast turned for me my mourning into dancing: thou hast put off my sackcloth, and girded me with gladness;

¹² To the end that my glory may sing praise to thee, and not be silent. O Lord my God, I will give thanks unto thee for ever.

Psalm 31

In thee, O Lord, do I put my trust; let me never be ashamed: deliver me in thy righteousness.

² Bow down thine ear to me; deliver me speedily: be thou my strong rock, for an house of defence to save me.

³ For thou art my rock and my fortress; therefore for thy name's sake lead me, and guide me.

⁴ Pull me out of the net that they have laid privily for me: for thou art my strength.

⁵ Into thine hand I commit my spirit: thou hast redeemed me, O Lord God of truth.

⁶ I have hated them that regard lying vanities: but I trust in the Lord.

⁷ I will be glad and rejoice in thy mercy: for thou hast considered my trouble; thou hast known my soul in adversities;

⁸ And hast not shut me up into the hand of the enemy: thou hast set my feet in a large room.

⁹ Have mercy upon me, O Lord, for I am in trouble: mine eye is consumed with grief, yea, my soul and my belly.

¹⁰ For my life is spent with grief, and my years with sighing: my strength faileth because of mine iniquity, and my bones are consumed.

¹¹ I was a reproach among all mine enemies, but especially among my neighbours, and a fear to mine acquaintance: they that did see me without fled from me.

¹² I am forgotten as a dead man out of mind: I am like a broken vessel.

[13] For I have heard the slander of many: fear was on every side: while they took counsel together against me, they devised to take away my life.

[14] But I trusted in thee, O Lord: I said, Thou art my God.

[15] My times are in thy hand: deliver me from the hand of mine enemies, and from them that persecute me.

[16] Make thy face to shine upon thy servant: save me for thy mercies' sake.

[17] Let me not be ashamed, O Lord; for I have called upon thee: let the wicked be ashamed, and let them be silent in the grave.

[18] Let the lying lips be put to silence; which speak grievous things proudly and contemptuously against the righteous.

[19] Oh how great is thy goodness, which thou hast laid up for them that fear thee; which thou hast wrought for them that trust in thee before the sons of men!

[20] Thou shalt hide them in the secret of thy presence from the pride of men: thou shalt keep them secretly in a pavilion from the strife of tongues.

[21] Blessed be the Lord: for he hath shewed me his marvellous kindness in a strong city.

[22] For I said in my haste, I am cut off from before thine eyes: nevertheless thou heardest the voice of my supplications when I cried unto thee.

[23] O love the Lord, all ye his saints: for the Lord preserveth the faithful, and plentifully rewardeth the proud doer.

[24] Be of good courage, and he shall strengthen your heart, all ye that hope in the Lord.

Psalm 32

Blessed is he whose transgression is forgiven, whose sin is covered.

² Blessed is the man unto whom the Lord imputeth not iniquity, and in whose spirit there is no guile.

³ When I kept silence, my bones waxed old through my roaring all the day long.

⁴ For day and night thy hand was heavy upon me: my moisture is turned into the drought of summer. Selah.

⁵ I acknowledged my sin unto thee, and mine iniquity have I not hid. I said, I will confess my transgressions unto the Lord; and thou forgavest the iniquity of my sin. Selah.

⁶ For this shall every one that is godly pray unto thee in a time when thou mayest be found: surely in the floods of great waters they shall not come nigh unto him.

⁷ Thou art my hiding place; thou shalt preserve me from trouble; thou shalt compass me about with songs of deliverance. Selah.

⁸ I will instruct thee and teach thee in the way which thou shalt go. I will guide thee with mine eye.

⁹ Be ye not as the horse, or as the mule, which have no understanding: whose mouth must be held in with bit and bridle, lest they come near unto thee.

¹⁰ Many sorrows shall be to the wicked: but he that trusteth in the Lord, mercy shall compass him about.

¹¹ Be glad in the Lord, and rejoice, ye righteous: and shout for joy, all ye that are upright in heart.

Psalm 33

Rejoice in the Lord, O ye righteous: for praise is comely for the upright.

² Praise the Lord with harp: sing unto him with the psaltery and an instrument of ten strings.

³ Sing unto him a new song; play skilfully with a loud noise.

[4] For the word of the Lord is right; and all his works are done in truth.

[5] He loveth righteousness and judgment: the earth is full of the goodness of the Lord.

[6] By the word of the Lord were the heavens made; and all the host of them by the breath of his mouth.

[7] He gathereth the waters of the sea together as an heap: he layeth up the depth in storehouses.

[8] Let all the earth fear the Lord: let all the inhabitants of the world stand in awe of him.

[9] For he spake, and it was done; he commanded, and it stood fast.

[10] The Lord bringeth the counsel of the heathen to nought: he maketh the devices of the people of none effect.

[11] The counsel of the Lord standeth for ever, the thoughts of his heart to all generations.

[12] Blessed is the nation whose God is the Lord; and the people whom he hath chosen for his own inheritance.

[13] The Lord looketh from heaven; he beholdeth all the sons of men.

[14] From the place of his habitation he looketh upon all the inhabitants of the earth.

[15] He fashioneth their hearts alike; he considereth all their works.

[16] There is no king saved by the multitude of an host: a mighty man is not delivered by much strength.

[17] An horse is a vain thing for safety: neither shall he deliver any by his great strength.

[18] Behold, the eye of the Lord is upon them that fear him, upon them that hope in his mercy;

¹⁹ To deliver their soul from death, and to keep them alive in famine.

²⁰ Our soul waiteth for the Lord: he is our help and our shield.

²¹ For our heart shall rejoice in him, because we have trusted in his holy name.

²² Let thy mercy, O Lord, be upon us, according as we hope in thee.

Psalm 34

I will bless the Lord at all times: his praise shall continually be in my mouth.

² My soul shall make her boast in the Lord: the humble shall hear thereof, and be glad.

³ O magnify the Lord with me, and let us exalt his name together.

⁴ I sought the Lord, and he heard me, and delivered me from all my fears.

⁵ They looked unto him, and were lightened: and their faces were not ashamed.

⁶ This poor man cried, and the Lord heard him, and saved him out of all his troubles.

⁷ The angel of the Lord encampeth round about them that fear him, and delivereth them.

⁸ O taste and see that the Lord is good: blessed is the man that trusteth in him.

⁹ O fear the Lord, ye his saints: for there is no want to them that fear him.

¹⁰ The young lions do lack and suffer hunger: but they that seek the Lord shall not want any good thing.

¹¹ Come, ye children, hearken unto me: I will teach you the fear of the Lord.

¹² What man is he that desireth life, and loveth many days, that he may see good?

¹³ Keep thy tongue from evil, and thy lips from speaking guile.

¹⁴ Depart from evil, and do good; seek peace, and pursue it.

¹⁵ The eyes of the Lord are upon the righteous, and his ears are open unto their cry.

¹⁶ The face of the Lord is against them that do evil, to cut off the remembrance of them from the earth.

¹⁷ The righteous cry, and the Lord heareth, and delivereth them out of all their troubles.

¹⁸ The Lord is nigh unto them that are of a broken heart; and saveth such as be of a contrite spirit.

¹⁹ Many are the afflictions of the righteous: but the Lord delivereth him out of them all.

²⁰ He keepeth all his bones: not one of them is broken.

²¹ Evil shall slay the wicked: and they that hate the righteous shall be desolate.

²² The Lord redeemeth the soul of his servants: and none of them that trust in him shall be desolate.

Psalm 35

Plead my cause, O Lord, with them that strive with me: fight against them that fight against me.

² Take hold of shield and buckler, and stand up for mine help.

³ Draw out also the spear, and stop the way against them that persecute me: say unto my soul, I am thy salvation.

⁴ Let them be confounded and put to shame that seek after my soul: let them be turned back and brought to confusion that devise my hurt.

⁵ Let them be as chaff before the wind: and let the angel of the Lord chase them.

⁶ Let their way be dark and slippery: and let the angel of the Lord persecute them.

⁷ For without cause have they hid for me their net in a pit, which without cause they have digged for my soul.

⁸ Let destruction come upon him at unawares; and let his net that he hath hid catch himself: into that very destruction let him fall.

⁹ And my soul shall be joyful in the Lord: it shall rejoice in his salvation.

¹⁰ All my bones shall say, Lord, who is like unto thee, which deliverest the poor from him that is too strong for him, yea, the poor and the needy from him that spoileth him?

¹¹ False witnesses did rise up; they laid to my charge things that I knew not.

¹² They rewarded me evil for good to the spoiling of my soul.

¹³ But as for me, when they were sick, my clothing was sackcloth: I humbled my soul with fasting; and my prayer returned into mine own bosom.

¹⁴ I behaved myself as though he had been my friend or brother: I bowed down heavily, as one that mourneth for his mother.

¹⁵ But in mine adversity they rejoiced, and gathered themselves together: yea, the abjects gathered themselves together against me, and I knew it not; they did tear me, and ceased not:

¹⁶ With hypocritical mockers in feasts, they gnashed upon me with their teeth.

[17] Lord, how long wilt thou look on? rescue my soul from their destructions, my darling from the lions.

[18] I will give thee thanks in the great congregation: I will praise thee among much people.

[19] Let not them that are mine enemies wrongfully rejoice over me: neither let them wink with the eye that hate me without a cause.

[20] For they speak not peace: but they devise deceitful matters against them that are quiet in the land.

[21] Yea, they opened their mouth wide against me, and said, Aha, aha, our eye hath seen it.

[22] This thou hast seen, O Lord: keep not silence: O Lord, be not far from me.

[23] Stir up thyself, and awake to my judgment, even unto my cause, my God and my Lord.

[24] Judge me, O Lord my God, according to thy righteousness; and let them not rejoice over me.

[25] Let them not say in their hearts, Ah, so would we have it: let them not say, We have swallowed him up.

[26] Let them be ashamed and brought to confusion together that rejoice at mine hurt: let them be clothed with shame and dishonour that magnify themselves against me.

[27] Let them shout for joy, and be glad, that favour my righteous cause: yea, let them say continually, Let the Lord be magnified, which hath pleasure in the prosperity of his servant.

[28] And my tongue shall speak of thy righteousness and of thy praise all the day long.

Psalm 36

The transgression of the wicked saith within my heart, that there is no fear of God before his eyes.

² For he flattereth himself in his own eyes, until his iniquity be found to be hateful.

³ The words of his mouth are iniquity and deceit: he hath left off to be wise, and to do good.

⁴ He deviseth mischief upon his bed; he setteth himself in a way that is not good; he abhorreth not evil.

⁵ Thy mercy, O Lord, is in the heavens; and thy faithfulness reacheth unto the clouds.

⁶ Thy righteousness is like the great mountains; thy judgments are a great deep: O Lord, thou preservest man and beast.

⁷ How excellent is thy lovingkindness, O God! therefore the children of men put their trust under the shadow of thy wings.

⁸ They shall be abundantly satisfied with the fatness of thy house; and thou shalt make them drink of the river of thy pleasures.

⁹ For with thee is the fountain of life: in thy light shall we see light.

¹⁰ O continue thy lovingkindness unto them that know thee; and thy righteousness to the upright in heart.

¹¹ Let not the foot of pride come against me, and let not the hand of the wicked remove me.

¹² There are the workers of iniquity fallen: they are cast down, and shall not be able to rise.

Psalm 37

Fret not thyself because of evildoers, neither be thou envious against the workers of iniquity.

² For they shall soon be cut down like the grass, and wither as the green herb.

³ Trust in the Lord, and do good; so shalt thou dwell in the land, and verily thou shalt be fed.

⁴ Delight thyself also in the Lord; and he shall give thee the desires of thine heart.

⁵ Commit thy way unto the Lord; trust also in him; and he shall bring it to pass.

⁶ And he shall bring forth thy righteousness as the light, and thy judgment as the noonday.

⁷ Rest in the Lord, and wait patiently for him: fret not thyself because of him who prospereth in his way, because of the man who bringeth wicked devices to pass.

⁸ Cease from anger, and forsake wrath: fret not thyself in any wise to do evil.

⁹ For evildoers shall be cut off: but those that wait upon the Lord, they shall inherit the earth.

¹⁰ For yet a little while, and the wicked shall not be: yea, thou shalt diligently consider his place, and it shall not be.

¹¹ But the meek shall inherit the earth; and shall delight themselves in the abundance of peace.

¹² The wicked plotteth against the just, and gnasheth upon him with his teeth.

¹³ The Lord shall laugh at him: for he seeth that his day is coming.

¹⁴ The wicked have drawn out the sword, and have bent their bow, to cast down the poor and needy, and to slay such as be of upright conversation.

¹⁵ Their sword shall enter into their own heart, and their bows shall be broken.

¹⁶ A little that a righteous man hath is better than the riches of many wicked.

¹⁷ For the arms of the wicked shall be broken: but the Lord upholdeth the righteous.

¹⁸ The Lord knoweth the days of the upright: and their inheritance shall be for ever.

¹⁹ They shall not be ashamed in the evil time: and in the days of famine they shall be satisfied.

²⁰ But the wicked shall perish, and the enemies of the Lord shall be as the fat of lambs: they shall consume; into smoke shall they consume away.

²¹ The wicked borroweth, and payeth not again: but the righteous sheweth mercy, and giveth.

²² For such as be blessed of him shall inherit the earth; and they that be cursed of him shall be cut off.

²³ The steps of a good man are ordered by the Lord: and he delighteth in his way.

²⁴ Though he fall, he shall not be utterly cast down: for the Lord upholdeth him with his hand.

²⁵ I have been young, and now am old; yet have I not seen the righteous forsaken, nor his seed begging bread.

²⁶ He is ever merciful, and lendeth; and his seed is blessed.

²⁷ Depart from evil, and do good; and dwell for evermore.

²⁸ For the Lord loveth judgment, and forsaketh not his saints; they are preserved for ever: but the seed of the wicked shall be cut off.

²⁹ The righteous shall inherit the land, and dwell therein for ever.

³⁰ The mouth of the righteous speaketh wisdom, and his tongue talketh of judgment.

³¹ The law of his God is in his heart; none of his steps shall slide.

³² The wicked watcheth the righteous, and seeketh to slay him.

³³ The Lord will not leave him in his hand, nor condemn him when he is judged.

[34] Wait on the Lord, and keep his way, and he shall exalt thee to inherit the land: when the wicked are cut off, thou shalt see it.

[35] I have seen the wicked in great power, and spreading himself like a green bay tree.

[36] Yet he passed away, and, lo, he was not: yea, I sought him, but he could not be found.

[37] Mark the perfect man, and behold the upright: for the end of that man is peace.

[38] But the transgressors shall be destroyed together: the end of the wicked shall be cut off.

[39] But the salvation of the righteous is of the Lord: he is their strength in the time of trouble.

[40] And the Lord shall help them, and deliver them: he shall deliver them from the wicked, and save them, because they trust in him.

Psalm 38

O Lord, rebuke me not in thy wrath: neither chasten me in thy hot displeasure.

[2] For thine arrows stick fast in me, and thy hand presseth me sore.

[3] There is no soundness in my flesh because of thine anger; neither is there any rest in my bones because of my sin.

[4] For mine iniquities are gone over mine head: as an heavy burden they are too heavy for me.

[5] My wounds stink and are corrupt because of my foolishness.

[6] I am troubled; I am bowed down greatly; I go mourning all the day long.

[7] For my loins are filled with a loathsome disease: and there is no soundness in my flesh.

[8] I am feeble and sore broken: I have roared by reason of the disquietness of my heart.

9 Lord, all my desire is before thee; and my groaning is not hid from thee.

10 My heart panteth, my strength faileth me: as for the light of mine eyes, it also is gone from me.

11 My lovers and my friends stand aloof from my sore; and my kinsmen stand afar off.

12 They also that seek after my life lay snares for me: and they that seek my hurt speak mischievous things, and imagine deceits all the day long.

13 But I, as a deaf man, heard not; and I was as a dumb man that openeth not his mouth.

14 Thus I was as a man that heareth not, and in whose mouth are no reproofs.

15 For in thee, O Lord, do I hope: thou wilt hear, O Lord my God.

16 For I said, Hear me, lest otherwise they should rejoice over me: when my foot slippeth, they magnify themselves against me.

17 For I am ready to halt, and my sorrow is continually before me.

18 For I will declare mine iniquity; I will be sorry for my sin.

19 But mine enemies are lively, and they are strong: and they that hate me wrongfully are multiplied.

20 They also that render evil for good are mine adversaries; because I follow the thing that good is.

21 Forsake me not, O Lord: O my God, be not far from me.

22 Make haste to help me, O Lord my salvation.

Psalm 39

I said, I will take heed to my ways, that I sin not with my tongue: I will keep my mouth with a bridle, while the wicked is before me.

² I was dumb with silence, I held my peace, even from good; and my sorrow was stirred.

³ My heart was hot within me, while I was musing the fire burned: then spake I with my tongue,

⁴ Lord, make me to know mine end, and the measure of my days, what it is; that I may know how frail I am.

⁵ Behold, thou hast made my days as an handbreadth; and mine age is as nothing before thee: verily every man at his best state is altogether vanity. Selah.

⁶ Surely every man walketh in a vain shew: surely they are disquieted in vain: he heapeth up riches, and knoweth not who shall gather them.

⁷ And now, Lord, what wait I for? my hope is in thee.

⁸ Deliver me from all my transgressions: make me not the reproach of the foolish.

⁹ I was dumb, I opened not my mouth; because thou didst it.

¹⁰ Remove thy stroke away from me: I am consumed by the blow of thine hand.

¹¹ When thou with rebukes dost correct man for iniquity, thou makest his beauty to consume away like a moth: surely every man is vanity. Selah.

¹² Hear my prayer, O Lord, and give ear unto my cry; hold not thy peace at my tears: for I am a stranger with thee, and a sojourner, as all my fathers were.

¹³ O spare me, that I may recover strength, before I go hence, and be no more.

Psalm 40

I waited patiently for the Lord; and he inclined unto me, and heard my cry.

² He brought me up also out of an horrible pit, out of the miry clay, and set my feet upon a rock, and established my goings.

³ And he hath put a new song in my mouth, even praise unto our God: many shall see it, and fear, and shall trust in the Lord.

⁴ Blessed is that man that maketh the Lord his trust, and respecteth not the proud, nor such as turn aside to lies.

⁵ Many, O Lord my God, are thy wonderful works which thou hast done, and thy thoughts which are to us-ward: they cannot be reckoned up in order unto thee: if I would declare and speak of them, they are more than can be numbered.

⁶ Sacrifice and offering thou didst not desire; mine ears hast thou opened: burnt offering and sin offering hast thou not required.

⁷ Then said I, Lo, I come: in the volume of the book it is written of me,

⁸ I delight to do thy will, O my God: yea, thy law is within my heart.

⁹ I have preached righteousness in the great congregation: lo, I have not refrained my lips, O Lord, thou knowest.

¹⁰ I have not hid thy righteousness within my heart; I have declared thy faithfulness and thy salvation: I have not concealed thy lovingkindness and thy truth from the great congregation.

¹¹ Withhold not thou thy tender mercies from me, O Lord: let thy lovingkindness and thy truth continually preserve me.

¹² For innumerable evils have compassed me about: mine iniquities have taken hold upon me, so that I am not able to look up; they are more than the hairs of mine head: therefore my heart faileth me.

¹³ Be pleased, O Lord, to deliver me: O Lord, make haste to help me.

14 Let them be ashamed and confounded together that seek after my soul to destroy it; let them be driven backward and put to shame that wish me evil.

15 Let them be desolate for a reward of their shame that say unto me, Aha, aha.

16 Let all those that seek thee rejoice and be glad in thee: let such as love thy salvation say continually, The Lord be magnified.

17 But I am poor and needy; yet the Lord thinketh upon me: thou art my help and my deliverer; make no tarrying, O my God.

Psalm 41

Blessed is he that considereth the poor: the Lord will deliver him in time of trouble.

2 The Lord will preserve him, and keep him alive; and he shall be blessed upon the earth: and thou wilt not deliver him unto the will of his enemies.

3 The Lord will strengthen him upon the bed of languishing: thou wilt make all his bed in his sickness.

4 I said, Lord, be merciful unto me: heal my soul; for I have sinned against thee.

5 Mine enemies speak evil of me, When shall he die, and his name perish?

6 And if he come to see me, he speaketh vanity: his heart gathereth iniquity to itself; when he goeth abroad, he telleth it.

7 All that hate me whisper together against me: against me do they devise my hurt.

8 An evil disease, say they, cleaveth fast unto him: and now that he lieth he shall rise up no more.

9 Yea, mine own familiar friend, in whom I trusted, which did eat of my bread, hath lifted up his heel against me.

¹⁰ But thou, O Lord, be merciful unto me, and raise me up, that I may requite them.

¹¹ By this I know that thou favourest me, because mine enemy doth not triumph over me.

¹² And as for me, thou upholdest me in mine integrity, and settest me before thy face for ever.

¹³ Blessed be the Lord God of Israel from everlasting, and to everlasting. Amen, and Amen.

Psalm 42

As the hart panteth after the water brooks, so panteth my soul after thee, O God.

² My soul thirsteth for God, for the living God: when shall I come and appear before God?

³ My tears have been my meat day and night, while they continually say unto me, Where is thy God?

⁴ When I remember these things, I pour out my soul in me: for I had gone with the multitude, I went with them to the house of God, with the voice of joy and praise, with a multitude that kept holyday.

⁵ Why art thou cast down, O my soul? and why art thou disquieted in me? hope thou in God: for I shall yet praise him for the help of his countenance.

⁶ O my God, my soul is cast down within me: therefore will I remember thee from the land of Jordan, and of the Hermonites, from the hill Mizar.

⁷ Deep calleth unto deep at the noise of thy waterspouts: all thy waves and thy billows are gone over me.

⁸ Yet the Lord will command his lovingkindness in the daytime, and in the night his song shall be with me, and my prayer unto the God of my life.

⁹ I will say unto God my rock, Why hast thou forgotten me? why go I mourning because of the oppression of the enemy?

¹⁰ As with a sword in my bones, mine enemies reproach me; while they say daily unto me, Where is thy God?

¹¹ Why art thou cast down, O my soul? and why art thou disquieted within me? hope thou in God: for I shall yet praise him, who is the health of my countenance, and my God.

Psalm 43

Judge me, O God, and plead my cause against an ungodly nation: O deliver me from the deceitful and unjust man.

² For thou art the God of my strength: why dost thou cast me off? why go I mourning because of the oppression of the enemy?

³ O send out thy light and thy truth: let them lead me; let them bring me unto thy holy hill, and to thy tabernacles.

⁴ Then will I go unto the altar of God, unto God my exceeding joy: yea, upon the harp will I praise thee, O God my God.

⁵ Why art thou cast down, O my soul? and why art thou disquieted within me? hope in God: for I shall yet praise him, who is the health of my countenance, and my God.

Psalm 44

We have heard with our ears, O God, our fathers have told us, what work thou didst in their days, in the times of old.

² How thou didst drive out the heathen with thy hand, and plantedst them; how thou didst afflict the people, and cast them out.

³ For they got not the land in possession by their own sword, neither did their own arm save them: but thy right hand, and thine arm, and the light of thy countenance, because thou hadst a favour unto them.

⁴ Thou art my King, O God: command deliverances for Jacob.

⁵ Through thee will we push down our enemies: through thy name will we tread them under that rise up against us.

⁶ For I will not trust in my bow, neither shall my sword save me.

⁷ But thou hast saved us from our enemies, and hast put them to shame that hated us.

⁸ In God we boast all the day long, and praise thy name for ever. Selah.

⁹ But thou hast cast off, and put us to shame; and goest not forth with our armies.

¹⁰ Thou makest us to turn back from the enemy; and they which hate us spoil for themselves.

¹¹ Thou hast given us like sheep appointed for meat; and hast scattered us among the heathen.

¹² Thou sellest thy people for nought, and dost not increase thy wealth by their price.

¹³ Thou makest us a reproach to our neighbours, a scorn and a derision to them that are round about us.

¹⁴ Thou makest us a byword among the heathen, a shaking of the head among the people.

¹⁵ My confusion is continually before me, and the shame of my face hath covered me,

¹⁶ For the voice of him that reproacheth and blasphemeth; by reason of the enemy and avenger.

¹⁷ All this is come upon us; yet have we not forgotten thee, neither have we dealt falsely in thy covenant.

¹⁸ Our heart is not turned back neither have our steps declined from thy way;

¹⁹ Though thou hast sore broken us in the place of dragons, and covered us with the shadow of death.

²⁰ If we have forgotten the name of our God, or stretched out our hands to a strange god;

²¹ Shall not God search this out? for he knoweth the secrets of the heart.

²² Yea, for thy sake are we killed all the day long; we are counted as sheep for the slaughter.

²³ Awake, why sleepest thou, O Lord? arise, cast us not off for ever.

²⁴ Wherefore hidest thou thy face, and forgettest our affliction and our oppression?

²⁵ For our soul is bowed down to the dust: our belly cleaveth unto the earth.

²⁶ Arise for our help, and redeem us for thy mercies' sake.

Psalm 45

My heart is inditing a good matter: I speak of the things which I have made touching the king: my tongue is the pen of a ready writer.

² Thou art fairer than the children of men: grace is poured into thy lips: therefore God hath blessed thee for ever.

³ Gird thy sword upon thy thigh, O most mighty, with thy glory and thy majesty.

⁴ And in thy majesty ride prosperously because of truth and meekness and righteousness; and thy right hand shall teach thee terrible things.

⁵ Thine arrows are sharp in the heart of the king's enemies; whereby the people fall under thee.

⁶ Thy throne, O God, is for ever and ever: the sceptre of thy kingdom is a right sceptre.

⁷ Thou lovest righteousness, and hatest wickedness: therefore God, thy God, hath anointed thee with the oil of gladness above thy fellows.

⁸ All thy garments smell of myrrh, and aloes, and cassia, out of the ivory palaces, whereby they have made thee glad.

⁹ Kings' daughters were among thy honourable women: upon thy right hand did stand the queen in gold of Ophir.

¹⁰ Hearken, O daughter, and consider, and incline thine ear; forget also thine own people, and thy father's house;

¹¹ So shall the king greatly desire thy beauty: for he is thy Lord; and worship thou him.

¹² And the daughter of Tyre shall be there with a gift; even the rich among the people shall intreat thy favour.

¹³ The king's daughter is all glorious within: her clothing is of wrought gold.

¹⁴ She shall be brought unto the king in raiment of needlework: the virgins her companions that follow her shall be brought unto thee.

¹⁵ With gladness and rejoicing shall they be brought: they shall enter into the king's palace.

¹⁶ Instead of thy fathers shall be thy children, whom thou mayest make princes in all the earth.

¹⁷ I will make thy name to be remembered in all generations: therefore shall the people praise thee for ever and ever.

Psalm 46

God is our refuge and strength, a very present help in trouble.

² Therefore will not we fear, though the earth be removed, and though the mountains be carried into the midst of the sea;

³ Though the waters thereof roar and be troubled, though the mountains shake with the swelling thereof. Selah.

⁴ There is a river, the streams whereof shall make glad the city of God, the holy place of the tabernacles of the most High.

⁵ God is in the midst of her; she shall not be moved: God shall help her, and that right early.

⁶ The heathen raged, the kingdoms were moved: he uttered his voice, the earth melted.

⁷ The Lord of hosts is with us; the God of Jacob is our refuge. Selah.

⁸ Come, behold the works of the Lord, what desolations he hath made in the earth.

⁹ He maketh wars to cease unto the end of the earth; he breaketh the bow, and cutteth the spear in sunder; he burneth the chariot in the fire.

¹⁰ Be still, and know that I am God: I will be exalted among the heathen, I will be exalted in the earth.

¹¹ The Lord of hosts is with us; the God of Jacob is our refuge. Selah.

Psalm 47

O clap your hands, all ye people; shout unto God with the voice of triumph.

² For the Lord most high is terrible; he is a great King over all the earth.

³ He shall subdue the people under us, and the nations under our feet.

⁴ He shall choose our inheritance for us, the excellency of Jacob whom he loved. Selah.

⁵ God is gone up with a shout, the Lord with the sound of a trumpet.

⁶ Sing praises to God, sing praises: sing praises unto our King, sing praises.

⁷ For God is the King of all the earth: sing ye praises with understanding.

⁸ God reigneth over the heathen: God sitteth upon the throne of his holiness.

⁹ The princes of the people are gathered together, even the people of the God of Abraham: for the shields of the earth belong unto God: he is greatly exalted.

Psalm 48

Great is the Lord, and greatly to be praised in the city of our God, in the mountain of his holiness.

² Beautiful for situation, the joy of the whole earth, is mount Zion, on the sides of the north, the city of the great King.

³ God is known in her palaces for a refuge.

⁴ For, lo, the kings were assembled, they passed by together.

⁵ They saw it, and so they marvelled; they were troubled, and hasted away.

⁶ Fear took hold upon them there, and pain, as of a woman in travail.

⁷ Thou breakest the ships of Tarshish with an east wind.

⁸ As we have heard, so have we seen in the city of the Lord of hosts, in the city of our God: God will establish it for ever. Selah.

⁹ We have thought of thy lovingkindness, O God, in the midst of thy temple.

¹⁰ According to thy name, O God, so is thy praise unto the ends of the earth: thy right hand is full of righteousness.

¹¹ Let mount Zion rejoice, let the daughters of Judah be glad, because of thy judgments.

¹² Walk about Zion, and go round about her: tell the towers thereof.

¹³ Mark ye well her bulwarks, consider her palaces; that ye may tell it to the generation following.

¹⁴ For this God is our God for ever and ever: he will be our guide even unto death.

Psalm 49

Hear this, all ye people; give ear, all ye inhabitants of the world:

² Both low and high, rich and poor, together.

³ My mouth shall speak of wisdom; and the meditation of my heart shall be of understanding.

⁴ I will incline mine ear to a parable: I will open my dark saying upon the harp.

⁵ Wherefore should I fear in the days of evil, when the iniquity of my heels shall compass me about?

⁶ They that trust in their wealth, and boast themselves in the multitude of their riches;

⁷ None of them can by any means redeem his brother, nor give to God a ransom for him:

⁸ (For the redemption of their soul is precious, and it ceaseth for ever:)

⁹ That he should still live for ever, and not see corruption.

¹⁰ For he seeth that wise men die, likewise the fool and the brutish person perish, and leave their wealth to others.

¹¹ Their inward thought is, that their houses shall continue for ever, and their dwelling places to all generations; they call their lands after their own names.

¹² Nevertheless man being in honour abideth not: he is like the beasts that perish.

¹³ This their way is their folly: yet their posterity approve their sayings. Selah.

[14] Like sheep they are laid in the grave; death shall feed on them; and the upright shall have dominion over them in the morning; and their beauty shall consume in the grave from their dwelling.

[15] But God will redeem my soul from the power of the grave: for he shall receive me. Selah.

[16] Be not thou afraid when one is made rich, when the glory of his house is increased;

[17] For when he dieth he shall carry nothing away: his glory shall not descend after him.

[18] Though while he lived he blessed his soul: and men will praise thee, when thou doest well to thyself.

[19] He shall go to the generation of his fathers; they shall never see light.

[20] Man that is in honour, and understandeth not, is like the beasts that perish.

Psalm 50

The mighty God, even the Lord, hath spoken, and called the earth from the rising of the sun unto the going down thereof.

[2] Out of Zion, the perfection of beauty, God hath shined.

[3] Our God shall come, and shall not keep silence: a fire shall devour before him, and it shall be very tempestuous round about him.

[4] He shall call to the heavens from above, and to the earth, that he may judge his people.

[5] Gather my saints together unto me; those that have made a covenant with me by sacrifice.

[6] And the heavens shall declare his righteousness: for God is judge himself. Selah.

[7] Hear, O my people, and I will speak; O Israel, and I will testify against thee: I am God, even thy God.

[8] I will not reprove thee for thy sacrifices or thy burnt offerings, to have been continually before me.

[9] I will take no bullock out of thy house, nor he goats out of thy folds.

[10] For every beast of the forest is mine, and the cattle upon a thousand hills.

[11] I know all the fowls of the mountains: and the wild beasts of the field are mine.

[12] If I were hungry, I would not tell thee: for the world is mine, and the fulness thereof.

[13] Will I eat the flesh of bulls, or drink the blood of goats?

[14] Offer unto God thanksgiving; and pay thy vows unto the most High:

[15] And call upon me in the day of trouble: I will deliver thee, and thou shalt glorify me.

[16] But unto the wicked God saith, What hast thou to do to declare my statutes, or that thou shouldest take my covenant in thy mouth?

[17] Seeing thou hatest instruction, and castest my words behind thee.

[18] When thou sawest a thief, then thou consentedst with him, and hast been partaker with adulterers.

[19] Thou givest thy mouth to evil, and thy tongue frameth deceit.

[20] Thou sittest and speakest against thy brother; thou slanderest thine own mother's son.

[21] These things hast thou done, and I kept silence; thou thoughtest that I was altogether such an one as thyself: but I will reprove thee, and set them in order before thine eyes.

[22] Now consider this, ye that forget God, lest I tear you in pieces, and there be none to deliver.

²³ Whoso offereth praise glorifieth me: and to him that ordereth his conversation aright will I shew the salvation of God.

Psalm 51

Have mercy upon me, O God, according to thy lovingkindness: according unto the multitude of thy tender mercies blot out my transgressions.

² Wash me throughly from mine iniquity, and cleanse me from my sin.

³ For I acknowledge my transgressions: and my sin is ever before me.

⁴ Against thee, thee only, have I sinned, and done this evil in thy sight: that thou mightest be justified when thou speakest, and be clear when thou judgest.

⁵ Behold, I was shapen in iniquity; and in sin did my mother conceive me.

⁶ Behold, thou desirest truth in the inward parts: and in the hidden part thou shalt make me to know wisdom.

⁷ Purge me with hyssop, and I shall be clean: wash me, and I shall be whiter than snow.

⁸ Make me to hear joy and gladness; that the bones which thou hast broken may rejoice.

⁹ Hide thy face from my sins, and blot out all mine iniquities.

¹⁰ Create in me a clean heart, O God; and renew a right spirit within me.

¹¹ Cast me not away from thy presence; and take not thy holy spirit from me.

¹² Restore unto me the joy of thy salvation; and uphold me with thy free spirit.

¹³ Then will I teach transgressors thy ways; and sinners shall be converted unto thee.

¹⁴ Deliver me from bloodguiltiness, O God, thou God of my salvation: and my tongue shall sing aloud of thy righteousness.

¹⁵ O Lord, open thou my lips; and my mouth shall shew forth thy praise.

¹⁶ For thou desirest not sacrifice; else would I give it: thou delightest not in burnt offering.

¹⁷ The sacrifices of God are a broken spirit: a broken and a contrite heart, O God, thou wilt not despise.

¹⁸ Do good in thy good pleasure unto Zion: build thou the walls of Jerusalem.

¹⁹ Then shalt thou be pleased with the sacrifices of righteousness, with burnt offering and whole burnt offering: then shall they offer bullocks upon thine altar.

Psalm 52

Why boastest thou thyself in mischief, O mighty man? the goodness of God endureth continually.

² Thy tongue deviseth mischiefs; like a sharp razor, working deceitfully.

³ Thou lovest evil more than good; and lying rather than to speak righteousness. Selah.

⁴ Thou lovest all devouring words, O thou deceitful tongue.

⁵ God shall likewise destroy thee for ever, he shall take thee away and pluck thee out of thy dwelling place, and root thee out of the land of the living. Selah.

⁶ The righteous also shall see, and fear, and shall laugh at him:

⁷ Lo, this is the man that made not God his strength; but trusted in the abundance of his riches, and strengthened himself in his wickedness.

⁸ But I am like a green olive tree in the house of God: I trust in the mercy of God for ever and ever.

⁹ I will praise thee for ever, because thou hast done it: and I will wait on thy name; for it is good before thy saints.

Psalm 53

The fool hath said in his heart, There is no God. Corrupt are they, and have done abominable iniquity: there is none that doeth good.

² God looked down from heaven upon the children of men, to see if there were any that did understand, that did seek God.

³ Every one of them is gone back: they are altogether become filthy; there is none that doeth good, no, not one.

⁴ Have the workers of iniquity no knowledge? who eat up my people as they eat bread: they have not called upon God.

⁵ There were they in great fear, where no fear was: for God hath scattered the bones of him that encampeth against thee: thou hast put them to shame, because God hath despised them.

⁶ Oh that the salvation of Israel were come out of Zion! When God bringeth back the captivity of his people, Jacob shall rejoice, and Israel shall be glad.

Psalm 54

Save me, O God, by thy name, and judge me by thy strength.

² Hear my prayer, O God; give ear to the words of my mouth.

³ For strangers are risen up against me, and oppressors seek after my soul: they have not set God before them. Selah.

⁴ Behold, God is mine helper: the Lord is with them that uphold my soul.

[5] He shall reward evil unto mine enemies: cut them off in thy truth.

[6] I will freely sacrifice unto thee: I will praise thy name, O Lord; for it is good.

[7] For he hath delivered me out of all trouble: and mine eye hath seen his desire upon mine enemies.

Psalm 55

Give ear to my prayer, O God; and hide not thyself from my supplication.

[2] Attend unto me, and hear me: I mourn in my complaint, and make a noise;

[3] Because of the voice of the enemy, because of the oppression of the wicked: for they cast iniquity upon me, and in wrath they hate me.

[4] My heart is sore pained within me: and the terrors of death are fallen upon me.

[5] Fearfulness and trembling are come upon me, and horror hath overwhelmed me.

[6] And I said, Oh that I had wings like a dove! for then would I fly away, and be at rest.

[7] Lo, then would I wander far off, and remain in the wilderness. Selah.

[8] I would hasten my escape from the windy storm and tempest.

[9] Destroy, O Lord, and divide their tongues: for I have seen violence and strife in the city.

[10] Day and night they go about it upon the walls thereof: mischief also and sorrow are in the midst of it.

[11] Wickedness is in the midst thereof: deceit and guile depart not from her streets.

[12] For it was not an enemy that reproached me; then I could have borne it: neither was it he that hated me that did magnify himself against me; then I would have hid myself from him:

[13] But it was thou, a man mine equal, my guide, and mine acquaintance.

[14] We took sweet counsel together, and walked unto the house of God in company.

[15] Let death seize upon them, and let them go down quick into hell: for wickedness is in their dwellings, and among them.

[16] As for me, I will call upon God; and the Lord shall save me.

[17] Evening, and morning, and at noon, will I pray, and cry aloud: and he shall hear my voice.

[18] He hath delivered my soul in peace from the battle that was against me: for there were many with me.

[19] God shall hear, and afflict them, even he that abideth of old. Selah. Because they have no changes, therefore they fear not God.

[20] He hath put forth his hands against such as be at peace with him: he hath broken his covenant.

[21] The words of his mouth were smoother than butter, but war was in his heart: his words were softer than oil, yet were they drawn swords.

[22] Cast thy burden upon the Lord, and he shall sustain thee: he shall never suffer the righteous to be moved.

[23] But thou, O God, shalt bring them down into the pit of destruction: bloody and deceitful men shall not live out half their days; but I will trust in thee.

Psalm 56

Be merciful unto me, O God: for man would swallow me up; he fighting daily oppresseth me.

² Mine enemies would daily swallow me up: for they be many that fight against me, O thou most High.

³ What time I am afraid, I will trust in thee.

⁴ In God I will praise his word, in God I have put my trust; I will not fear what flesh can do unto me.

⁵ Every day they wrest my words: all their thoughts are against me for evil.

⁶ They gather themselves together, they hide themselves, they mark my steps, when they wait for my soul.

⁷ Shall they escape by iniquity? in thine anger cast down the people, O God.

⁸ Thou tellest my wanderings: put thou my tears into thy bottle: are they not in thy book?

⁹ When I cry unto thee, then shall mine enemies turn back: this I know; for God is for me.

¹⁰ In God will I praise his word: in the Lord will I praise his word.

¹¹ In God have I put my trust: I will not be afraid what man can do unto me.

¹² Thy vows are upon me, O God: I will render praises unto thee.

¹³ For thou hast delivered my soul from death: wilt not thou deliver my feet from falling, that I may walk before God in the light of the living?

Psalm 57

Be merciful unto me, O God, be merciful unto me: for my soul trusteth in thee: yea, in the shadow of thy wings will I make my refuge, until these calamities be overpast.

² I will cry unto God most high; unto God that performeth all things for me.

³ He shall send from heaven, and save me from the reproach of him that would swallow me up. Selah. God shall send forth his mercy and his truth.

⁴ My soul is among lions: and I lie even among them that are set on fire, even the sons of men, whose teeth are spears and arrows, and their tongue a sharp sword.

⁵ Be thou exalted, O God, above the heavens; let thy glory be above all the earth.

⁶ They have prepared a net for my steps; my soul is bowed down: they have digged a pit before me, into the midst whereof they are fallen themselves. Selah.

⁷ My heart is fixed, O God, my heart is fixed: I will sing and give praise.

⁸ Awake up, my glory; awake, psaltery and harp: I myself will awake early.

⁹ I will praise thee, O Lord, among the people: I will sing unto thee among the nations.

¹⁰ For thy mercy is great unto the heavens, and thy truth unto the clouds.

¹¹ Be thou exalted, O God, above the heavens: let thy glory be above all the earth.

Psalm 58

Do ye indeed speak righteousness, O congregation? do ye judge uprightly, O ye sons of men?

² Yea, in heart ye work wickedness; ye weigh the violence of your hands in the earth.

³ The wicked are estranged from the womb: they go astray as soon as they be born, speaking lies.

⁴ Their poison is like the poison of a serpent: they are like the deaf adder that stoppeth her ear;

⁵ Which will not hearken to the voice of charmers, charming never so wisely.

⁶ Break their teeth, O God, in their mouth: break out the great teeth of the young lions, O Lord.

⁷ Let them melt away as waters which run continually: when he bendeth his bow to shoot his arrows, let them be as cut in pieces.

⁸ As a snail which melteth, let every one of them pass away: like the untimely birth of a woman, that they may not see the sun.

⁹ Before your pots can feel the thorns, he shall take them away as with a whirlwind, both living, and in his wrath.

¹⁰ The righteous shall rejoice when he seeth the vengeance: he shall wash his feet in the blood of the wicked.

¹¹ So that a man shall say, Verily there is a reward for the righteous: verily he is a God that judgeth in the earth.

Psalm 59

Deliver me from mine enemies, O my God: defend me from them that rise up against me.

² Deliver me from the workers of iniquity, and save me from bloody men.

³ For, lo, they lie in wait for my soul: the mighty are gathered against me; not for my transgression, nor for my sin, O Lord.

⁴ They run and prepare themselves without my fault: awake to help me, and behold.

⁵ Thou therefore, O Lord God of hosts, the God of Israel, awake to visit all the heathen: be not merciful to any wicked transgressors. Selah.

⁶ They return at evening: they make a noise like a dog, and go round about the city.

⁷ Behold, they belch out with their mouth: swords are in their lips: for who, say they, doth hear?

⁸ But thou, O Lord, shalt laugh at them; thou shalt have all the heathen in derision.

⁹ Because of his strength will I wait upon thee: for God is my defence.

¹⁰ The God of my mercy shall prevent me: God shall let me see my desire upon mine enemies.

¹¹ Slay them not, lest my people forget: scatter them by thy power; and bring them down, O Lord our shield.

¹² For the sin of their mouth and the words of their lips let them even be taken in their pride: and for cursing and lying which they speak.

¹³ Consume them in wrath, consume them, that they may not be: and let them know that God ruleth in Jacob unto the ends of the earth. Selah.

¹⁴ And at the evening let them return; and let them make a noise like a dog, and go round about the city.

¹⁵ Let them wander up and down for meat, and grudge if they be not satisfied.

¹⁶ But I will sing of thy power; yea, I will sing aloud of thy mercy in the morning: for thou hast been my defence and refuge in the day of my trouble.

¹⁷ Unto thee, O my strength, will I sing: for God is my defence, and the God of my mercy.

Psalm 60

O God, thou hast cast us off, thou hast scattered us, thou hast been displeased; O turn thyself to us again.

² Thou hast made the earth to tremble; thou hast broken it: heal the breaches thereof; for it shaketh.

³ Thou hast shewed thy people hard things: thou hast made us to drink the wine of astonishment.

⁴ Thou hast given a banner to them that fear thee, that it may be displayed because of the truth. Selah.

⁵ That thy beloved may be delivered; save with thy right hand, and hear me.

⁶ God hath spoken in his holiness; I will rejoice, I will divide Shechem, and mete out the valley of Succoth.

⁷ Gilead is mine, and Manasseh is mine; Ephraim also is the strength of mine head; Judah is my lawgiver;

⁸ Moab is my washpot; over Edom will I cast out my shoe: Philistia, triumph thou because of me.

⁹ Who will bring me into the strong city? who will lead me into Edom?

¹⁰ Wilt not thou, O God, which hadst cast us off? and thou, O God, which didst not go out with our armies?

¹¹ Give us help from trouble: for vain is the help of man.

¹² Through God we shall do valiantly: for he it is that shall tread down our enemies.

Psalm 61

Hear my cry, O God; attend unto my prayer.

² From the end of the earth will I cry unto thee, when my heart is overwhelmed: lead me to the rock that is higher than I.

³ For thou hast been a shelter for me, and a strong tower from the enemy.

⁴ I will abide in thy tabernacle for ever: I will trust in the covert of thy wings. Selah.

⁵ For thou, O God, hast heard my vows: thou hast given me the heritage of those that fear thy name.

⁶ Thou wilt prolong the king's life: and his years as many generations.

⁷ He shall abide before God for ever: O prepare mercy and truth, which may preserve him.

⁸ So will I sing praise unto thy name for ever, that I may daily perform my vows.

Psalm 62

Truly my soul waiteth upon God: from him cometh my salvation.

² He only is my rock and my salvation; he is my defence; I shall not be greatly moved.

³ How long will ye imagine mischief against a man? ye shall be slain all of you: as a bowing wall shall ye be, and as a tottering fence.

⁴ They only consult to cast him down from his excellency: they delight in lies: they bless with their mouth, but they curse inwardly. Selah.

⁵ My soul, wait thou only upon God; for my expectation is from him.

⁶ He only is my rock and my salvation: he is my defence; I shall not be moved.

⁷ In God is my salvation and my glory: the rock of my strength, and my refuge, is in God.

⁸ Trust in him at all times; ye people, pour out your heart before him: God is a refuge for us. Selah.

⁹ Surely men of low degree are vanity, and men of high degree are a lie: to be laid in the balance, they are altogether lighter than vanity.

¹⁰ Trust not in oppression, and become not vain in robbery: if riches increase, set not your heart upon them.

¹¹ God hath spoken once; twice have I heard this; that power belongeth unto God.

¹² Also unto thee, O Lord, belongeth mercy: for thou renderest to every man according to his work.

Psalm 63

O God, thou art my God; early will I seek thee: my soul thirsteth for thee, my flesh longeth for thee in a dry and thirsty land, where no water is;

² To see thy power and thy glory, so as I have seen thee in the sanctuary.

³ Because thy lovingkindness is better than life, my lips shall praise thee.

⁴ Thus will I bless thee while I live: I will lift up my hands in thy name.

⁵ My soul shall be satisfied as with marrow and fatness; and my mouth shall praise thee with joyful lips:

⁶ When I remember thee upon my bed, and meditate on thee in the night watches.

⁷ Because thou hast been my help, therefore in the shadow of thy wings will I rejoice.

⁸ My soul followeth hard after thee: thy right hand upholdeth me.

⁹ But those that seek my soul, to destroy it, shall go into the lower parts of the earth.

¹⁰ They shall fall by the sword: they shall be a portion for foxes.

¹¹ But the king shall rejoice in God; every one of them that speak lies shall be stopped.

Psalm 64

Hear my voice, O God, in my prayer: preserve my life from fear of the enemy.

² Hide me from the secret counsel of the wicked; from the insurrection of the workers of iniquity:

³ Who whet their tongue like a sword, and bend their bows to shoot their arrows, even bitter words:

⁴ That they may shoot in secret at the perfect: suddenly do they shoot at him, and fear not.

⁵ They encourage themselves in an evil matter: they commune of laying snares privily; they say, Who shall see them?

⁶ They search out iniquities; they accomplish a diligent search: both the inward thought of every one of them, and the heart, is deep.

⁷ But God shall shoot at them with an arrow; suddenly shall they be wounded.

⁸ So they shall make their own tongue to fall upon themselves: all that see them shall flee away.

⁹ And all men shall fear, and shall declare the work of God; for they shall wisely consider of his doing.

¹⁰ The righteous shall be glad in the Lord, and shall trust in him; and all the upright in heart shall glory.

Psalm 65

Praise waiteth for thee, O God, in Zion: and unto thee shall the vow be performed.

² O thou that hearest prayer, unto thee shall all flesh come.

³ Iniquities prevail against me: as for our transgressions, thou shalt purge them away.

[4] Blessed is the man whom thou choosest, and causest to approach unto thee, that he may dwell in thy courts: we shall be satisfied with the goodness of thy house, even of thy holy temple.

[5] By terrible things in righteousness wilt thou answer us, O God of our salvation; who art the confidence of all the ends of the earth, and of them that are afar off upon the sea:

[6] Which by his strength setteth fast the mountains; being girded with power:

[7] Which stilleth the noise of the seas, the noise of their waves, and the tumult of the people.

[8] They also that dwell in the uttermost parts are afraid at thy tokens: thou makest the outgoings of the morning and evening to rejoice.

[9] Thou visitest the earth, and waterest it: thou greatly enrichest it with the river of God, which is full of water: thou preparest them corn, when thou hast so provided for it.

[10] Thou waterest the ridges thereof abundantly: thou settlest the furrows thereof: thou makest it soft with showers: thou blessest the springing thereof.

[11] Thou crownest the year with thy goodness: and the little hills rejoice on every side.

[12] They drop upon the pastures of the wilderness: and the little hills rejoice on every side.

[13] The pastures are clothed with flocks; the valleys also are covered over with corn; they shout for joy, they also sing.

Psalm 66

Make a joyful noise unto God, all ye lands:

[2] Sing forth the honour of his name: make his praise glorious.

³ Say unto God, How terrible art thou in thy works! through the greatness of thy power shall thine enemies submit themselves unto thee.

⁴ All the earth shall worship thee, and shall sing unto thee; they shall sing to thy name. Selah.

⁵ Come and see the works of God: he is terrible in his doing toward the children of men.

⁶ He turned the sea into dry land: they went through the flood on foot: there did we rejoice in him.

⁷ He ruleth by his power for ever; his eyes behold the nations: let not the rebellious exalt themselves. Selah.

⁸ O bless our God, ye people, and make the voice of his praise to be heard:

⁹ Which holdeth our soul in life, and suffereth not our feet to be moved.

¹⁰ For thou, O God, hast proved us: thou hast tried us, as silver is tried.

¹¹ Thou broughtest us into the net; thou laidst affliction upon our loins.

¹² Thou hast caused men to ride over our heads; we went through fire and through water: but thou broughtest us out into a wealthy place.

¹³ I will go into thy house with burnt offerings: I will pay thee my vows,

¹⁴ Which my lips have uttered, and my mouth hath spoken, when I was in trouble.

¹⁵ I will offer unto thee burnt sacrifices of fatlings, with the incense of rams; I will offer bullocks with goats. Selah.

[16] Come and hear, all ye that fear God, and I will declare what he hath done for my soul.

[17] I cried unto him with my mouth, and he was extolled with my tongue.

[18] If I regard iniquity in my heart, the Lord will not hear me:

[19] But verily God hath heard me; he hath attended to the voice of my prayer.

[20] Blessed be God, which hath not turned away my prayer, nor his mercy from me.

Psalm 67

God be merciful unto us, and bless us; and cause his face to shine upon us; Selah.

[2] That thy way may be known upon earth, thy saving health among all nations.

[3] Let the people praise thee, O God; let all the people praise thee.

[4] O let the nations be glad and sing for joy: for thou shalt judge the people righteously, and govern the nations upon earth. Selah.

[5] Let the people praise thee, O God; let all the people praise thee.

[6] Then shall the earth yield her increase; and God, even our own God, shall bless us.

[7] God shall bless us; and all the ends of the earth shall fear him.

Psalm 68

Let God arise, let his enemies be scattered: let them also that hate him flee before him.

[2] As smoke is driven away, so drive them away: as wax melteth before the fire, so let the wicked perish at the presence of God.

[3] But let the righteous be glad; let them rejoice before God: yea, let them exceedingly rejoice.

⁴ Sing unto God, sing praises to his name: extol him that rideth upon the heavens by his name JÄH, and rejoice before him.

⁵ A father of the fatherless, and a judge of the widows, is God in his holy habitation.

⁶ God setteth the solitary in families: he bringeth out those which are bound with chains: but the rebellious dwell in a dry land.

⁷ O God, when thou wentest forth before thy people, when thou didst march through the wilderness; Selah:

⁸ The earth shook, the heavens also dropped at the presence of God: even Sinai itself was moved at the presence of God, the God of Israel.

⁹ Thou, O God, didst send a plentiful rain, whereby thou didst confirm thine inheritance, when it was weary.

¹⁰ Thy congregation hath dwelt therein: thou, O God, hast prepared of thy goodness for the poor.

¹¹ The Lord gave the word: great was the company of those that published it.

¹² Kings of armies did flee apace: and she that tarried at home divided the spoil.

¹³ Though ye have lien among the pots, yet shall ye be as the wings of a dove covered with silver, and her feathers with yellow gold.

¹⁴ When the Almighty scattered kings in it, it was white as snow in Salmon.

¹⁵ The hill of God is as the hill of Bashan; an high hill as the hill of Bashan.

¹⁶ Why leap ye, ye high hills? this is the hill which God desireth to dwell in; yea, the Lord will dwell in it for ever.

¹⁷ The chariots of God are twenty thousand, even thousands of angels: the Lord is among them, as in Sinai, in the holy place.

[18] Thou hast ascended on high, thou hast led captivity captive: thou hast received gifts for men; yea, for the rebellious also, that the Lord God might dwell among them.

[19] Blessed be the Lord, who daily loadeth us with benefits, even the God of our salvation. Selah,

[20] He that is our God is the God of salvation; and unto God the Lord belong the issues from death.

[21] But God shall wound the head of his enemies, and the hairy scalp of such an one as goeth on still in his trespasses.

[22] The Lord said, I will bring again from Bashan, I will bring my people again from the depths of the sea:

[23] That thy foot may be dipped in the blood of thine enemies, and the tongue of thy dogs in the same.

[24] They have seen thy goings, O God; even the goings of my God, my King, in the sanctuary.

[25] The singers went before, the players on instruments followed after; among them were the damsels playing with timbrels.

[26] Bless ye God in the congregations, even the Lord, from the fountain of Israel.

[27] There is little Benjamin with their ruler, the princes of Judah and their council, the princes of Zebulun, and the princes of Naphtali.

[28] Thy God hath commanded thy strength: strengthen, O God, that which thou hast wrought for us.

[29] Because of thy temple at Jerusalem shall kings bring presents unto thee.

[30] Rebuke the company of spearmen, the multitude of the bulls, with the calves of the people, till every one submit himself with pieces of silver: scatter thou the people that delight in war.

³¹ Princes shall come out of Egypt; Ethiopia shall soon stretch out her hands unto God.

³² Sing unto God, ye kingdoms of the earth; O sing praises unto the Lord; Selah:

³³ To him that rideth upon the heavens, which were of old; lo, he doth send out his voice, and that a mighty voice.

³⁴ Ascribe ye strength unto God: his excellency is over Israel, and his strength is in the clouds.

³⁵ O God, thou art terrible out of thy holy places: the God of Israel is he that giveth strength and power unto his people. Blessed be God.

Psalm 69

Save me, O God; for the waters are come in unto my soul.

² I sink in deep mire, where there is no standing: I am come into deep waters, where the floods overflow me.

³ I am weary of my crying: my throat is dried: mine eyes fail while I wait for my God.

⁴ They that hate me without a cause are more than the hairs of mine head: they that would destroy me, being mine enemies wrongfully, are mighty: then I restored that which I took not away.

⁵ O God, thou knowest my foolishness; and my sins are not hid from thee.

⁶ Let not them that wait on thee, O Lord God of hosts, be ashamed for my sake: let not those that seek thee be confounded for my sake, O God of Israel.

⁷ Because for thy sake I have borne reproach; shame hath covered my face.

⁸ I am become a stranger unto my brethren, and an alien unto my mother's children.

⁹ For the zeal of thine house hath eaten me up; and the reproaches of them that reproached thee are fallen upon me.

¹⁰ When I wept and chastened my soul with fasting, that was to my reproach.

¹¹ I made sackcloth also my garment; and I became a proverb to them.

¹² They that sit in the gate speak against me; and I was the song of the drunkards.

¹³ But as for me, my prayer is unto thee, O Lord, in an acceptable time: O God, in the multitude of thy mercy hear me, in the truth of thy salvation.

¹⁴ Deliver me out of the mire, and let me not sink: let me be delivered from them that hate me, and out of the deep waters.

¹⁵ Let not the waterflood overflow me, neither let the deep swallow me up, and let not the pit shut her mouth upon me.

¹⁶ Hear me, O Lord; for thy lovingkindness is good: turn unto me according to the multitude of thy tender mercies.

¹⁷ And hide not thy face from thy servant; for I am in trouble; hear me speedily.

¹⁸ Draw nigh unto my soul, and redeem it: deliver me because of mine enemies.

¹⁹ Thou hast known my reproach, and my shame, and my dishonour: mine adversaries are all before thee.

²⁰ Reproach hath broken my heart; and I am full of heaviness; and I looked for some to take pity, but there was none; and for comforters, but I found none.

²¹ They gave me also gall for my meat: and in my thirst they gave me vinegar to drink.

²² Let their table become a snare before them: and that which should have been for their welfare, let it become a trap.

²³ Let their eyes be darkened, that they see not; and make their loins continually to shake.

²⁴ Pour out thine indignation upon them, and let thy wrathful anger take hold of them.

²⁵ Let their habitation be desolate; and let none dwell in their tents.

²⁶ For they persecute him whom thou hast smitten; and they talk to the grief of those whom thou hast wounded.

²⁷ Add iniquity unto their iniquity: and let them not come into thy righteousness.

²⁸ Let them be blotted out of the book of the living, and not be written with the righteous.

²⁹ But I am poor and sorrowful: let thy salvation, O God, set me up on high.

³⁰ I will praise the name of God with a song, and will magnify him with thanksgiving.

³¹ This also shall please the Lord better than an ox or bullock that hath horns and hoofs.

³² The humble shall see this, and be glad: and your heart shall live that seek God.

³³ For the Lord heareth the poor, and despiseth not his prisoners.

³⁴ Let the heaven and earth praise him, the seas, and every thing that moveth therein.

³⁵ For God will save Zion and will build the cities of Judah: that they may dwell there, and have it in possession.

³⁶ The seed also of his servants shall inherit it: and they that love his name shall dwell therein.

Psalm 70

Make haste, O God to deliver me; make haste to help me, O Lord.

² Let them be ashamed and confounded that seek after my soul: let them be turned backward, and put to confusion, that desire my hurt.

³ Let them be turned back for a reward of their shame that say, Aha, aha.

⁴ Let all those that seek thee rejoice and be glad in thee: and let such as love thy salvation say continually, Let God be magnified.

⁵ But I am poor and needy: make haste unto me, O God: thou art my help and my deliverer; O Lord, make no tarrying.

Psalm 71

In thee, O Lord, do I put my trust: let me never be put to confusion.

² Deliver me in thy righteousness, and cause me to escape: incline thine ear unto me, and save me.

³ Be thou my stong habitation, whereunto I may continually resort: thou hast given commandment to save me; for thou art my rock and my fortress.

⁴ Deliver me, O my God, out of the hand of the wicked, out of the hand of the unrighteous and cruel man.

⁵ For thou art my hope, O Lord God: thou art my trust from my youth.

⁶ By thee have I been holden up from the womb: thou art he that took me out of my mother's bowels: my praise shall be continually of thee.

⁷ I am as a wonder unto many; but thou art my strong refuge.

⁸ Let my mouth be filled with thy praise and with thy honour all the day.

⁹ Cast me not off in the time of old age; forsake me not when my strength faileth.

¹⁰ For mine enemies speak against me; and they that lay wait for my soul take counsel together.

¹¹ Saying, God hath forsaken him: persecute and take him; for there is none to deliver him.

¹² O God, be not far from me: O my God, make haste for my help.

¹³ Let them be confounded and consumed that are adversaries to my soul; let them be covered with reproach and dishonour that seek my hurt.

¹⁴ But I will hope continually, and will yet praise thee more and more.

¹⁵ My mouth shall shew forth thy righteousness and thy salvation all the day; for I know not the numbers thereof.

¹⁶ I will go in the strength of the Lord God: I will make mention of thy righteousness, even of thine only.

¹⁷ O God, thou hast taught me from my youth: and hitherto have I declared thy wondrous works.

¹⁸ Now also when I am old and grayheaded, O God, forsake me not; until I have shewed thy strength unto this generation, and thy power to every one that is to come.

¹⁹ Thy righteousness also, O God, is very high, who hast done great things: O God, who is like unto thee!

²⁰ Thou, which hast shewed me great and sore troubles, shalt quicken me again, and shalt bring me up again from the depths of the earth.

²¹ Thou shalt increase my greatness, and comfort me on every side.

²² I will also praise thee with the psaltery, even thy truth, O my God: unto thee will I sing with the harp, O thou Holy One of Israel.

²³ My lips shall greatly rejoice when I sing unto thee; and my soul, which thou hast redeemed.

²⁴ My tongue also shall talk of thy righteousness all the day long: for they are confounded, for they are brought unto shame, that seek my hurt.

Psalm 72

Give the king thy judgments, O God, and thy righteousness unto the king's son.

² He shall judge thy people with righteousness, and thy poor with judgment.

³ The mountains shall bring peace to the people, and the little hills, by righteousness.

⁴ He shall judge the poor of the people, he shall save the children of the needy, and shall break in pieces the oppressor.

⁵ They shall fear thee as long as the sun and moon endure, throughout all generations.

⁶ He shall come down like rain upon the mown grass: as showers that water the earth.

⁷ In his days shall the righteous flourish; and abundance of peace so long as the moon endureth.

⁸ He shall have dominion also from sea to sea, and from the river unto the ends of the earth.

⁹ They that dwell in the wilderness shall bow before him; and his enemies shall lick the dust.

¹⁰ The kings of Tarshish and of the isles shall bring presents: the kings of Sheba and Seba shall offer gifts.

¹¹ Yea, all kings shall fall down before him: all nations shall serve him.

¹² For he shall deliver the needy when he crieth; the poor also, and him that hath no helper.

¹³ He shall spare the poor and needy, and shall save the souls of the needy.

¹⁴ He shall redeem their soul from deceit and violence: and precious shall their blood be in his sight.

¹⁵ And he shall live, and to him shall be given of the gold of Sheba: prayer also shall be made for him continually; and daily shall he be praised.

¹⁶ There shall be an handful of corn in the earth upon the top of the mountains; the fruit thereof shall shake like Lebanon: and they of the city shall flourish like grass of the earth.

¹⁷ His name shall endure for ever: his name shall be continued as long as the sun: and men shall be blessed in him: all nations shall call him blessed.

¹⁸ Blessed be the Lord God, the God of Israel, who only doeth wondrous things.

¹⁹ And blessed be his glorious name for ever: and let the whole earth be filled with his glory; Amen and Amen.

²⁰ The prayers of David the son of Jesse are ended.

Psalm 73

Truly God is good to Israel, even such as are of a clean heart.

² But as for me, my feet were almost gone; my steps had well nigh slipped.

³ For I was envious at the foolish, when I saw the prosperity of the wicked.

⁴ For there are no bands in their death: but their strength is firm.

⁵ They are not in trouble as other men; neither are they plagued like other men.

⁶ Therefore pride compasseth them about as a chain; violence covereth them as a garment.

⁷ Their eyes stand out with fatness: they have more than heart could wish.

⁸ They are corrupt, and speak wickedly concerning oppression: they speak loftily.

⁹ They set their mouth against the heavens, and their tongue walketh through the earth.

¹⁰ Therefore his people return hither: and waters of a full cup are wrung out to them.

¹¹ And they say, How doth God know? and is there knowledge in the most High?

¹² Behold, these are the ungodly, who prosper in the world; they increase in riches.

¹³ Verily I have cleansed my heart in vain, and washed my hands in innocency.

¹⁴ For all the day long have I been plagued, and chastened every morning.

¹⁵ If I say, I will speak thus; behold, I should offend against the generation of thy children.

¹⁶ When I thought to know this, it was too painful for me;

¹⁷ Until I went into the sanctuary of God; then understood I their end.

¹⁸ Surely thou didst set them in slippery places: thou castedst them down into destruction.

¹⁹ How are they brought into desolation, as in a moment! they are utterly consumed with terrors.

²⁰ As a dream when one awaketh; so, O Lord, when thou awakest, thou shalt despise their image.

²¹ Thus my heart was grieved and I was pricked in my reins.

²² So foolish was I, and ignorant: I was as a beast before thee.

²³ Nevertheless I am continually with thee: thou hast holden me by my right hand.

²⁴ Thou shalt guide me with thy counsel, and afterward receive me to glory.

²⁵ Whom have I in heaven but thee? and there is none upon earth that I desire beside thee.

²⁶ My flesh and my heart faileth: but God is the strength of my heart, and my portion for ever.

²⁷ For, lo, they that are far from thee shall perish: thou hast destroyed all them that go a whoring from thee.

²⁸ But it is good for me to draw near to God: I have put my trust in the Lord God, that I may declare all thy works.

Psalm 74

O God, why hast thou cast us off for ever? why doth thine anger smoke against the sheep of thy pasture?

² Remember thy congregation, which thou hast purchased of old; the rod of thine inheritance, which thou hast redeemed; this mount Zion, wherein thou hast dwelt.

³ Lift up thy feet unto the perpetual desolations; even all that the enemy hath done wickedly in the sanctuary.

⁴ Thine enemies roar in the midst of thy congregations; they set up their ensigns for signs.

⁵ A man was famous according as he had lifted up axes upon the thick trees.

⁶ But now they break down the carved work thereof at once with axes and hammers.

[7] They have cast fire into thy sanctuary, they have defiled by casting down the dwelling place of thy name to the ground.

[8] They said in their hearts, Let us destroy them together: they have burned up all the synagogues of God in the land.

[9] We see not our signs: there is no more any prophet: neither is there among us any that knoweth how long.

[10] O God, how long shall the adversary reproach? shall the enemy blaspheme thy name for ever?

[11] Why withdrawest thou thy hand, even thy right hand? pluck it out of thy bosom.

[12] For God is my king of old, working salvation in the midst of the earth.

[13] Thou didst divide the sea by thy strength: thou brakest the heads of the dragons in the waters.

[14] Thou brakest the heads of leviathan in pieces, and gavest him to be meat to the people inhabiting the wilderness.

[15] Thou didst cleave the fountain and the flood: thou driedst up mighty rivers.

[16] The day is thine, the night also is thine: thou hast prepared the light and the sun.

[17] Thou hast set all the borders of the earth: thou hast made summer and winter.

[18] Remember this, that the enemy hath reproached, O Lord, and that the foolish people have blasphemed thy name.

[19] O deliver not the soul of thy turtledove unto the multitude of the wicked: forget not the congregation of thy poor for ever.

[20] Have respect unto the covenant: for the dark places of the earth are full of the habitations of cruelty.

²¹ O let not the oppressed return ashamed: let the poor and needy praise thy name.

²² Arise, O God, plead thine own cause: remember how the foolish man reproacheth thee daily.

²³ Forget not the voice of thine enemies: the tumult of those that rise up against thee increaseth continually.

Psalm 75

Unto thee, O God, do we give thanks, unto thee do we give thanks: for that thy name is near thy wondrous works declare.

² When I shall receive the congregation I will judge uprightly.

³ The earth and all the inhabitants thereof are dissolved: I bear up the pillars of it. Selah.

⁴ I said unto the fools, Deal not foolishly: and to the wicked, Lift not up the horn:

⁵ Lift not up your horn on high: speak not with a stiff neck.

⁶ For promotion cometh neither from the east, nor from the west, nor from the south.

⁷ But God is the judge: he putteth down one, and setteth up another.

⁸ For in the hand of the Lord there is a cup, and the wine is red; it is full of mixture; and he poureth out of the same: but the dregs thereof, all the wicked of the earth shall wring them out, and drink them.

⁹ But I will declare forever; I will sing praises to the God of Jacob.

¹⁰ All the horns of the wicked also will I cut off; but the horns of the righteous shall be exalted.

Psalm 76

In Judah is God known: his name is great in Israel.

^{2} In Salem also is his tabernacle, and his dwelling place in Zion.

^{3} There brake he the arrows of the bow, the shield, and the sword, and the battle. Selah.

^{4} Thou art more glorious and excellent than the mountains of prey.

^{5} The stouthearted are spoiled, they have slept their sleep: and none of the men of might have found their hands.

^{6} At thy rebuke, O God of Jacob, both the chariot and horse are cast into a dead sleep.

^{7} Thou, even thou, art to be feared: and who may stand in thy sight when once thou art angry?

^{8} Thou didst cause judgment to be heard from heaven; the earth feared, and was still,

^{9} When God arose to judgment, to all the meek of the earth. Selah.

^{10} Surely the wrath of man shall praise thee: the remainder of wrath shalt thou restrain.

^{11} Vow, and pay unto the Lord your God: let all that be round about him bring presents unto him that ought to be feared.

^{12} He shall cut off the spirit of princes: he is terrible to the kings of the earth.

Psalm 77

I cried unto God with my voice, even unto God with my voice; and he gave ear unto me.

^{2} In the day of my trouble I sought the Lord: my sore ran in the night, and ceased not: my soul refused to be comforted.

^{3} I remembered God, and was troubled: I complained, and my spirit was overwhelmed. Selah.

⁴ Thou holdest mine eyes waking: I am so troubled that I cannot speak.

⁵ I have considered the days of old, the years of ancient times.

⁶ I call to remembrance my song in the night: I commune with mine own heart: and my spirit made diligent search.

⁷ Will the Lord cast off for ever? and will he be favourable no more?

⁸ Is his mercy clean gone for ever? doth his promise fail for evermore?

⁹ Hath God forgotten to be gracious? hath he in anger shut up his tender mercies? Selah.

¹⁰ And I said, This is my infirmity: but I will remember the years of the right hand of the most High.

¹¹ I will remember the works of the Lord: surely I will remember thy wonders of old.

¹² I will meditate also of all thy work, and talk of thy doings.

¹³ Thy way, O God, is in the sanctuary: who is so great a God as our God?

¹⁴ Thou art the God that doest wonders: thou hast declared thy strength among the people.

¹⁵ Thou hast with thine arm redeemed thy people, the sons of Jacob and Joseph. Selah.

¹⁶ The waters saw thee, O God, the waters saw thee; they were afraid: the depths also were troubled.

¹⁷ The clouds poured out water: the skies sent out a sound: thine arrows also went abroad.

¹⁸ The voice of thy thunder was in the heaven: the lightnings lightened the world: the earth trembled and shook.

¹⁹ Thy way is in the sea, and thy path in the great waters, and thy footsteps are not known.

²⁰ Thou leddest thy people like a flock by the hand of Moses and Aaron.

Psalm 78

Give ear, O my people, to my law: incline your ears to the words of my mouth.

² I will open my mouth in a parable: I will utter dark sayings of old:

³ Which we have heard and known, and our fathers have told us.

⁴ We will not hide them from their children, shewing to the generation to come the praises of the Lord, and his strength, and his wonderful works that he hath done.

⁵ For he established a testimony in Jacob, and appointed a law in Israel, which he commanded our fathers, that they should make them known to their children.

⁶ That the generation to come might know them, even the children which should be born; who should arise and declare them to their children.

⁷ That they might set their hope in God, and not forget the works of God, but keep his commandments.

⁸ And might not be as their fathers, a stubborn and rebellious generation; a generation that set not their heart aright, and whose spirit was not stedfast with God.

⁹ The children of Ephraim, being armed, and carrying bows, turned back in the day of battle.

¹⁰ They kept not the covenant of God, and refused to walk in his law.

¹¹ And forgat his works, and his wonders that he had shewed them.

¹² Marvellous things did he in the sight of their fathers, in the land of Egypt, in the field of Zoan.

¹³ He divided the sea, and caused them to pass through; and he made the waters to stand as an heap.

¹⁴ In the daytime also he led them with a cloud, and all the night with a light of fire.

¹⁵ He clave the rocks in the wilderness, and gave them drink as out of the great depths.

¹⁶ He brought streams also out of the rock, and caused waters to run down like rivers.

¹⁷ And they sinned yet more against him by provoking the most High in the wilderness.

¹⁸ And they tempted God in their heart by asking meat for their lust.

¹⁹ Yea, they spake against God; they said, Can God furnish a table in the wilderness?

²⁰ Behold, he smote the rock, that the waters gushed out, and the streams overflowed; can he give bread also? can he provide flesh for his people?

²¹ Therefore the Lord heard this, and was wroth: so a fire was kindled against Jacob, and anger also came up against Israel;

²² Because they believed not in God, and trusted not in his salvation:

²³ Though he had commanded the clouds from above, and opened the doors of heaven,

²⁴ And had rained down manna upon them to eat, and had given them of the corn of heaven.

²⁵ Man did eat angels' food: he sent them meat to the full.

²⁶ He caused an east wind to blow in the heaven: and by his power he brought in the south wind.

²⁷ He rained flesh also upon them as dust, and feathered fowls like as the sand of the sea:

²⁸ And he let it fall in the midst of their camp, round about their habitations.

²⁹ So they did eat, and were well filled: for he gave them their own desire;

³⁰ They were not estranged from their lust. But while their meat was yet in their mouths,

³¹ The wrath of God came upon them, and slew the fattest of them, and smote down the chosen men of Israel.

³² For all this they sinned still, and believed not for his wondrous works.

³³ Therefore their days did he consume in vanity, and their years in trouble.

³⁴ When he slew them, then they sought him: and they returned and inquired early after God.

³⁵ And they remembered that God was their rock, and the high God their redeemer.

³⁶ Nevertheless they did flatter him with their mouth, and they lied unto him with their tongues.

³⁷ For their heart was not right with him, neither were they stedfast in his covenant.

³⁸ But he, being full of compassion, forgave their iniquity, and destroyed them not: yea, many a time turned he his anger away, and did not stir up all his wrath.

³⁹ For he remembered that they were but flesh; a wind that passeth away, and cometh not again.

⁴⁰ How oft did they provoke him in the wilderness, and grieve him in the desert!

⁴¹ Yea, they turned back and tempted God, and limited the Holy One of Israel.

⁴² They remembered not his hand, nor the day when he delivered them from the enemy.

⁴³ How he had wrought his signs in Egypt, and his wonders in the field of Zoan.

⁴⁴ And had turned their rivers into blood; and their floods, that they could not drink.

⁴⁵ He sent divers sorts of flies among them, which devoured them; and frogs, which destroyed them.

⁴⁶ He gave also their increase unto the caterpiller, and their labour unto the locust.

⁴⁷ He destroyed their vines with hail, and their sycomore trees with frost.

⁴⁸ He gave up their cattle also to the hail, and their flocks to hot thunderbolts.

⁴⁹ He cast upon them the fierceness of his anger, wrath, and indignation, and trouble, by sending evil angels among them.

⁵⁰ He made a way to his anger; he spared not their soul from death, but gave their life over to the pestilence;

⁵¹ And smote all the firstborn in Egypt; the chief of their strength in the tabernacles of Ham:

⁵² But made his own people to go forth like sheep, and guided them in the wilderness like a flock.

⁵³ And he led them on safely, so that they feared not: but the sea overwhelmed their enemies.

⁵⁴ And he brought them to the border of his sanctuary, even to this mountain, which his right hand had purchased.

⁵⁵ He cast out the heathen also before them, and divided them an inheritance by line, and made the tribes of Israel to dwell in their tents.

⁵⁶ Yet they tempted and provoked the most high God, and kept not his testimonies.

⁵⁷ But turned back, and dealt unfaithfully like their fathers: they were turned aside like a deceitful bow.

⁵⁸ For they provoked him to anger with their high places, and moved him to jealousy with their graven images.

⁵⁹ When God heard this, he was wroth, and greatly abhorred Israel.

⁶⁰ So that he forsook the tabernacle of Shiloh, the tent which he placed among men;

⁶¹ And delivered his strength into captivity, and his glory into the enemy's hand.

⁶² He gave his people over also unto the sword; and was wroth with his inheritance.

⁶³ The fire consumed their young men; and their maidens were not given to marriage.

⁶⁴ Their priests fell by the sword; and their widows made no lamentation.

⁶⁵ Then the Lord awaked as one out of sleep, and like a mighty man that shouteth by reason of wine.

⁶⁶ And he smote his enemies in the hinder parts: he put them to a perpetual reproach.

⁶⁷ Moreover he refused the tabernacle of Joseph, and chose not the tribe of Ephraim:

⁶⁸ But chose the tribe of Judah, the mount Zion which he loved.

[69] And he built his sanctuary like high palaces, like the earth which he hath established for ever.

[70] He chose David also his servant, and took him from the sheepfolds:

[71] From following the ewes great with young he brought them to feed Jacob his people, and Israel his inheritance.

[72] So he fed them according to the integrity of his heart; and guided them by the skilfulness of his hands.

Psalm 79

O God, the heathen are come into thine inheritance; thy holy temple have they defiled; they have laid Jerusalem on heaps.

[2] The dead bodies of thy servants have they given to be meat unto the fowls of the heaven, the flesh of thy saints unto the beasts of the earth.

[3] Their blood have they shed like water round about Jerusalem; and there was none to bury them.

[4] We are become a reproach to our neighbours, a scorn and derision to them that are round about us.

[5] How long, Lord? wilt thou be angry for ever? shall thy jealousy burn like fire?

[6] Pour out thy wrath upon the heathen that have not known thee, and upon the kingdoms that have not called upon thy name.

[7] For they have devoured Jacob, and laid waste his dwelling place.

[8] O remember not against us former iniquities: let thy tender mercies speedily prevent us: for we are brought very low.

[9] Help us, O God of our salvation, for the glory of thy name: and deliver us, and purge away our sins, for thy name's sake.

[10] Wherefore should the heaven say, Where is their God? let him be known among the heathen in our sight by the revenging of the blood of thy servants which is shed.

[11] Let the sighing of the prisoner come before thee: according to the greatness of thy power preserve thou those that are appointed to die;

[12] And render unto our neighbours sevenfold into their bosom their reproach, wherewith they have reproached thee, O Lord.

[13] So we thy people and sheep of thy pasture will give thee thanks for ever: we will shew forth thy praise to all generations.

Psalm 80

Give ear, O Shepherd of Israel, thou that leadest Joseph like a flock; thou that dwellest between the cherubims, shine forth.

[2] Before Ephraim and Benjamin and Manasseh stir up thy strength, and come and save us.

[3] Turn us again, O God, and cause thy face to shine; and we shall be saved.

[4] O Lord God of hosts, how long wilt thou be angry against the prayer of thy people?

[5] Thou feedest them with the bread of tears; and givest them tears to drink in great measure.

[6] Thou makest us a strife unto our neighbours: and our enemies laugh among themselves.

[7] Turn us again, O God of hosts, and cause thy face to shine; and we shall be saved.

[8] Thou hast brought a vine out of Egypt: thou hast cast out the heathen, and planted it.

[9] Thou preparedst room before it, and didst cause it to take deep root, and it filled the land.

[10] The hills were covered with the shadow of it, and the boughs thereof were like the goodly cedars.

¹¹ She sent out her boughs unto the sea, and her branches unto the river.

¹² Why hast thou then broken down her hedges, so that all they which pass by the way do pluck her?

¹³ The boar out of the wood doth waste it, and the wild beast of the field doth devour it.

¹⁴ Return, we beseech thee, O God of hosts: look down from heaven, and behold, and visit this vine;

¹⁵ And the vineyard which thy right hand hath planted, and the branch that thou madest strong for thyself.

¹⁶ It is burned with fire, it is cut down: they perish at the rebuke of thy countenance.

¹⁷ Let thy hand be upon the man of thy right hand, upon the son of man whom thou madest strong for thyself.

¹⁸ So will not we go back from thee: quicken us, and we will call upon thy name.

¹⁹ Turn us again, O Lord God of hosts, cause thy face to shine; and we shall be saved.

Psalm 81

Sing aloud unto God our strength: make a joyful noise unto the God of Jacob.

² Take a psalm, and bring hither the timbrel, the pleasant harp with the psaltery.

³ Blow up the trumpet in the new moon, in the time appointed, on our solemn feast day.

⁴ For this was a statute for Israel, and a law of the God of Jacob.

⁵ This he ordained in Joseph for a testimony, when he went out through the land of Egypt: where I heard a language that I understood not.

⁶ I removed his shoulder from the burden: his hands were delivered from the pots.

⁷ Thou calledst in trouble, and I delivered thee; I answered thee in the secret place of thunder: I proved thee at the waters of Meribah. Selah.

⁸ Hear, O my people, and I will testify unto thee: O Israel, if thou wilt hearken unto me;

⁹ There shall no strange god be in thee; neither shalt thou worship any strange god.

¹⁰ I am the Lord thy God, which brought thee out of the land of Egypt: open thy mouth wide, and I will fill it.

¹¹ But my people would not hearken to my voice; and Israel would none of me.

¹² So I gave them up unto their own hearts lust: and they walked in their own counsels.

¹³ Oh that my people had hearkened unto me, and Israel had walked in my ways!

¹⁴ I should soon have subdued their enemies, and turned my hand against their adversaries,

¹⁵ The haters of the Lord should have submitted themselves unto him: but their time should have endured for ever.

¹⁶ He should have fed them also with the finest of the wheat: and with honey out of the rock should I have satisfied thee.

Psalm 82

God standeth in the congregation of the mighty; he judgeth among the gods.

² How long will ye judge unjustly, and accept the persons of the wicked? Selah.

³ Defend the poor and fatherless: do justice to the afflicted and needy.

⁴ Deliver the poor and needy: rid them out of the hand of the wicked.

⁵ They know not, neither will they understand; they walk on in darkness: all the foundations of the earth are out of course.

⁶ I have said, Ye are gods; and all of you are children of the most High.

⁷ But ye shall die like men, and fall like one of the princes.

⁸ Arise, O God, judge the earth: for thou shalt inherit all nations.

Psalm 83

Keep not thou silence, O God: hold not thy peace, and be not still, O God.

² For, lo, thine enemies make a tumult: and they that hate thee have lifted up the head.

³ They have taken crafty counsel against thy people, and consulted against thy hidden ones.

⁴ They have said, Come, and let us cut them off from being a nation; that the name of Israel may be no more in remembrance.

⁵ For they have consulted together with one consent: they are confederate against thee:

⁶ The tabernacles of Edom, and the Ishmaelites; of Moab and the Hagarenes;

⁷ Gebal, and Ammon, and Amalek; the Philistines with the inhabitants of Tyre;

⁸ Assur also is joined with them: they have holpen the children of Lot. Selah.

⁹ Do unto them as unto the Midianites; as to Sisera, as to Jabin, at the brook of Kison:

¹⁰ Which perished at Endor: they became as dung for the earth.

¹¹ Make their nobles like Oreb, and like Zeeb: yea, all their princes as Zebah, and as Zalmunna:

¹² Who said, Let us take to ourselves the houses of God in possession.

¹³ O my God, make them like a wheel; as the stubble before the wind.

¹⁴ As the fire burneth a wood, and as the flame setteth the mountains on fire;

¹⁵ So persecute them with thy tempest, and make them afraid with thy storm.

¹⁶ Fill their faces with shame; that they may seek thy name, O Lord.

¹⁷ Let them be confounded and troubled for ever; yea, let them be put to shame, and perish:

¹⁸ That men may know that thou, whose name alone is JEHOVAH, art the most high over all the earth.

Psalm 84

How amiable are thy tabernacles, O Lord of hosts!

² My soul longeth, yea, even fainteth for the courts of the Lord: my heart and my flesh crieth out for the living God.

³ Yea, the sparrow hath found an house, and the swallow a nest for herself, where she may lay her young, even thine altars, O Lord of hosts, my King and my God.

⁴ Blessed are they that dwell in thy house: they will be still praising thee. Selah.

⁵ Blessed is the man whose strength is in thee; in whose heart are the ways of them.

⁶ Who passing through the valley of Baca make it a well; the rain also filleth the pools.

⁷ They go from strength to strength, every one of them in Zion appeareth before God.

⁸ O Lord God of hosts, hear my prayer: give ear, O God of Jacob. Selah.

⁹ Behold, O God our shield, and look upon the face of thine anointed.

¹⁰ For a day in thy courts is better than a thousand. I had rather be a doorkeeper in the house of my God, then to dwell in the tents of wickedness.

¹¹ For the Lord God is a sun and shield: the Lord will give grace and glory: no good thing will he withhold from them that walk uprightly.

¹² O Lord of hosts, blessed is the man that trusteth in thee.

Psalm 85

Lord, thou hast been favourable unto thy land: thou hast brought back the captivity of Jacob.

² Thou hast forgiven the iniquity of thy people, thou hast covered all their sin. Selah.

³ Thou hast taken away all thy wrath: thou hast turned thyself from the fierceness of thine anger.

⁴ Turn us, O God of our salvation, and cause thine anger toward us to cease.

⁵ Wilt thou be angry with us for ever? wilt thou draw out thine anger to all generations?

⁶ Wilt thou not revive us again: that thy people may rejoice in thee?

⁷ Shew us thy mercy, O Lord, and grant us thy salvation.

⁸ I will hear what God the Lord will speak: for he will speak peace unto his people, and to his saints: but let them not turn again to folly.

⁹ Surely his salvation is nigh them that fear him; that glory may dwell in our land.

¹⁰ Mercy and truth are met together; righteousness and peace have kissed each other.

¹¹ Truth shall spring out of the earth; and righteousness shall look down from heaven.

¹² Yea, the Lord shall give that which is good; and our land shall yield her increase.

¹³ Righteousness shall go before him; and shall set us in the way of his steps.

Psalm 86

Bow down thine ear, O Lord, hear me; for I am poor and needy.

² Preserve my soul; for I am holy: O thou my God, save thy servant that trusteth in thee.

³ Be merciful unto me, O Lord: for I cry unto thee daily.

⁴ Rejoice the soul of thy servant: for unto thee, O Lord, do I lift up my soul.

⁵ For thou, Lord, art good, and ready to forgive; and plenteous in mercy unto all them that call upon thee.

⁶ Give ear, O Lord, unto my prayer; and attend to the voice of my supplications.

⁷ In the day of my trouble I will call upon thee: for thou wilt answer me.

⁸ Among the gods there is none like unto thee, O Lord; neither are there any works like unto thy works.

⁹ All nations whom thou hast made shall come and worship before thee, O Lord; and shall glorify thy name.

¹⁰ For thou art great, and doest wondrous things: thou art God alone.

¹¹ Teach me thy way, O Lord; I will walk in thy truth: unite my heart to fear thy name.

¹² I will praise thee, O Lord my God, with all my heart: and I will glorify thy name for evermore.

¹³ For great is thy mercy toward me: and thou hast delivered my soul from the lowest hell.

¹⁴ O God, the proud are risen against me, and the assemblies of violent men have sought after my soul; and have not set thee before them.

¹⁵ But thou, O Lord, art a God full of compassion, and gracious, longsuffering, and plenteous in mercy and truth.

¹⁶ O turn unto me, and have mercy upon me; give thy strength unto thy servant, and save the son of thine handmaid.

¹⁷ Shew me a token for good: that they which hate me may see it and be ashamed: because thou, Lord, hast holpen me, and comforted me.

Psalm 87

His foundation is in the holy mountains.

² The Lord loveth the gates of Zion more than all the dwellings of Jacob.

³ Glorious things are spoken of thee, O city of God. Selah.

[4] I will make mention of Rahab and Babylon to them that know me: behold Philistia and Tyre, with Ethiopia; this man was born there.

[5] And of Zion it shall be said, This and that man was born in her: and the highest himself shall establish her.

[6] The Lord shall count, when he writeth up the people, that this man was born there. Selah.

[7] As well the singers as the players on instruments shall be there: all my springs are in thee.

Psalm 88

O Lord God of my salvation, I have cried day and night before thee.

[2] Let my prayer come before thee: incline thine ear unto my cry;

[3] For my soul is full of troubles: and my life draweth nigh unto the grave.

[4] I am counted with them that go down into the pit: I am as a man that hath no strength:

[5] Free among the dead, like the slain that lie in the grave, whom thou rememberest no more: and they are cut off from thy hand.

[6] Thou hast laid me in the lowest pit, in darkness, in the deeps.

[7] Thy wrath lieth hard upon me, and thou hast afflicted me with all thy waves. Selah.

[8] Thou hast put away mine acquaintance far from me; thou hast made me an abomination unto them: I am shut up, and I cannot come forth.

[9] Mine eye mourneth by reason of affliction: Lord, I have called daily upon thee, I have stretched out my hands unto thee.

[10] Wilt thou shew wonders to the dead? shall the dead arise and praise thee? Selah.

¹¹ Shall thy lovingkindness be declared in the grave? or thy faithfulness in destruction?

¹² Shall thy wonders be known in the dark? and thy righteousness in the land of forgetfulness?

¹³ But unto thee have I cried, O Lord; and in the morning shall my prayer prevent thee.

¹⁴ Lord, why castest thou off my soul? why hidest thou thy face from me?

¹⁵ I am afflicted and ready to die from my youth up: while I suffer thy terrors I am distracted.

¹⁶ Thy fierce wrath goeth over me; thy terrors have cut me off.

¹⁷ They came round about me daily like water; they compassed me about together.

¹⁸ Lover and friend hast thou put far from me, and mine acquaintance into darkness.

Psalm 89

I will sing of the mercies of the Lord for ever: with my mouth will I make known thy faithfulness to all generations.

² For I have said, Mercy shall be built up for ever: thy faithfulness shalt thou establish in the very heavens.

³ I have made a convenant with my chosen, I have sworn unto David my servant,

⁴ Thy seed will I establish for ever, and build up thy throne to all generations. Selah.

⁵ And the heavens shall praise thy wonders, O Lord: thy faithfulness also in the congregation of the saints.

⁶ For who in the heaven can be compared unto the Lord? who among the sons of the mighty can be likened unto the Lord?

[7] God is greatly to be feared in the assembly of the saints, and to be had in reverence of all them that are about him.

[8] O Lord God of hosts, who is a strong Lord like unto thee? or to thy faithfulness round about thee?

[9] Thou rulest the raging of the sea: when the waves thereof arise, thou stillest them.

[10] Thou hast broken Rahab in pieces, as one that is slain; thou hast scattered thine enemies with thine strong arm,

[11] The heavens are thine, the earth also is thine: as for the world and the fulness thereof, thou hast founded them.

[12] The north and the south, thou hast created them: Tabor and Hermon shall rejoice in thy name.

[13] Thou hast a mighty arm: strong is thy hand, and high is thy right hand.

[14] Justice and judgment are the habitation of thy throne: mercy and truth shall go before thy face.

[15] Blessed is the people that know the joyful sound: they shall walk, O Lord, in the light of thy countenance.

[16] In thy name shall they rejoice all the day: and in thy righteousness shall they be exalted.

[17] For thou art the glory of their strength: and in thy favour our horn shall be exalted.

[18] For the Lord is our defence; and the Holy One of Israel is our king.

[19] Then thou spakest in vision to thy holy one, and saidst, I have laid help upon one that is mighty; I have exalted one chosen out of the people.

[20] I have found David my servant; with my holy oil have I anointed him.

[21] With whom my hand shall be established: mine arm also shall strengthen him,

[22] The enemy shall not exact upon him; nor the son of wickedness afflict him.

[23] And I will beat down his foes before his face, and plague them that hate him.

[24] But my faithfulness and my mercy shall be with him: and in my name shall his horn be exalted.

[25] I will set his hand also in the sea, and his right hand in the rivers.

[26] He shall cry unto me, Thou art my father, my God, and the rock of my salvation.

[27] Also I will make him my firstborn, higher than the kings of the earth.

[28] My mercy will I keep for him for evermore, and my covenant shall stand fast with him.

[29] His seed also will I make to endure for ever, and his throne as the days of heaven.

[30] If his children forsake my law, and walk not in my judgments;

[31] If they break my statutes, and keep not my commandments;

[32] Then will I visit their transgression with the rod, and their iniquity with stripes.

[33] Nevertheless my lovingkindness will I not utterly take from him, nor suffer my faithfulness to fail.

[34] My covenant will I not break, nor alter the thing that is gone out of my lips.

[35] Once have I sworn by my holiness that I will not lie unto David.

[36] His seed shall endure for ever, and his throne as the sun before me.

[37] It shall be established for ever as the moon, and as a faithful witness in heaven. Selah.

[38] But thou hast cast off and abhorred, thou hast been wroth with thine anointed.

[39] Thou has made void the covenant of thy servant: thou hast profaned his crown by casting it to the ground.

[40] Thou hast broken down all his hedges; thou hast brought his strong holds to ruin.

[41] All that pass by the way spoil him: he is a reproach to his neighbours.

[42] Thou hast set up the right hand of his adversaries; thou hast made all his enemies to rejoice.

[43] Thou hast also turned the edge of his sword, and hast not made him to stand in the battle.

[44] Thou hast made his glory to cease, and cast his throne down to the ground.

[45] The days of his youth hast thou shortened: thou hast covered him with shame. Selah.

[46] How long, Lord? wilt thou hide thyself for ever? shall thy wrath burn like fire?

[47] Remember how short my time is: wherefore hast thou made all men in vain?

[48] What man is he that liveth, and shall not see death? shall he deliver his soul from the hand of the grave? Selah.

[49] Lord, where are thy former lovingkindnesses, which thou swarest unto David in thy truth?

[50] Remember, Lord, the reproach of thy servants; how I do bear in my bosom the reproach of all the mighty people;

51 Wherewith thine enemies have reproached, O Lord; wherewith they have reproached the footsteps of thine anointed.

52 Blessed be the Lord for evermore. Amen and Amen.

Psalm 90

Lord, thou hast been our dwelling place in all generations.

2 Before the mountains were brought forth, or ever thou hadst formed the earth and the world, even from everlasting to everlasting, thou art God.

3 Thou turnest man to destruction; and sayest, Return, ye children of men.

4 For a thousand years in thy sight are but as yesterday when it is past, and as a watch in the night.

5 Thou carriest them away as with a flood; they are as a sleep: in the morning they are like grass which groweth up.

6 In the morning it flourisheth, and groweth up; in the evening it is cut down, and withereth.

7 For we are consumed by thine anger, and by thy wrath are we troubled.

8 Thou hast set our iniquities before thee, our secret sins in the light of thy countenance.

9 For all our days are passed away in thy wrath: we spend our years as a tale that is told.

10 The days of our years are threescore years and ten; and if by reason of strength they be fourscore years, yet is their strength labour and sorrow; for it is soon cut off, and we fly away.

11 Who knoweth the power of thine anger? even according to thy fear, so is thy wrath.

12 So teach us to number our days, that we may apply our hearts unto wisdom.

¹³ Return, O Lord, how long? and let it repent thee concerning thy servants.

¹⁴ O satisfy us early with thy mercy; that we may rejoice and be glad all our days.

¹⁵ Make us glad according to the days wherein thou hast afflicted us, and the years wherein we have seen evil.

¹⁶ Let thy work appear unto thy servants, and thy glory unto their children.

¹⁷ And let the beauty of the Lord our God be upon us; and establish thou the work of our hands upon us; yea, the work of our hands establish thou it.

Psalm 91

He that dwelleth in the secret place of the most High shall abide under the shadow of the Almighty.

² I will say of the Lord, He is my refuge and my fortress: my God; in him will I trust.

³ Surely he shall deliver thee from the snare of the fowler, and from the noisome pestilence.

⁴ He shall cover thee with his feathers, and under his wings shalt thou trust: his truth shall be thy shield and buckler.

⁵ Thou shalt not be afraid for the terror by night; nor for the arrow that flieth by day;

⁶ Nor for the pestilence that walketh in darkness; nor for the destruction that wasteth at noonday.

⁷ A thousand shall fall at thy side, and ten thousand at thy right hand; but it shall not come nigh thee.

⁸ Only with thine eyes shalt thou behold and see the reward of the wicked.

⁹ Because thou hast made the Lord, which is my refuge, even the most High, thy habitation;

¹⁰ There shall no evil befall thee, neither shall any plague come nigh thy dwelling.

¹¹ For he shall give his angels charge over thee, to keep thee in all thy ways.

¹² They shall bear thee up in their hands, lest thou dash thy foot against a stone.

¹³ Thou shalt tread upon the lion and adder: the young lion and the dragon shalt thou trample under feet.

¹⁴ Because he hath set his love upon me, therefore will I deliver him: I will set him on high, because he hath known my name.

¹⁵ He shall call upon me, and I will answer him: I will be with him in trouble; I will deliver him, and honour him.

¹⁶ With long life will I satisfy him, and shew him my salvation.

Psalm 92

It is a good thing to give thanks unto the Lord, and to sing praises unto thy name, O most High:

² To shew forth thy lovingkindness in the morning, and thy faithfulness every night,

³ Upon an instrument of ten strings, and upon the psaltery; upon the harp with a solemn sound.

⁴ For thou, Lord, hast made me glad through thy work: I will triumph in the works of thy hands.

⁵ O Lord, how great are thy works! and thy thoughts are very deep.

⁶ A brutish man knoweth not; neither doth a fool understand this.

⁷ When the wicked spring as the grass, and when all the workers of iniquity do flourish; it is that they shall be destroyed for ever:

[8] But thou, Lord, art most high for evermore.

[9] For, lo, thine enemies, O Lord, for, lo, thine enemies shall perish; all the workers of iniquity shall be scattered.

[10] But my horn shalt thou exalt like the horn of an unicorn: I shall be anointed with fresh oil.

[11] Mine eye also shall see my desire on mine enemies, and mine ears shall hear my desire of the wicked that rise up against me.

[12] The righteous shall flourish like the palm tree: he shall grow like a cedar in Lebanon.

[13] Those that be planted in the house of the Lord shall flourish in the courts of our God.

[14] They shall still bring forth fruit in old age; they shall be fat and flourishing;

[15] To shew that the Lord is upright: he is my rock, and there is no unrighteousness in him.

Psalm 93

The Lord reigneth, he is clothed with majesty; the Lord is clothed with strength, wherewith he hath girded himself; the world also is stablished, that it cannot be moved.

[2] Thy throne is established of old: thou art from everlasting.

[3] The floods have lifted up, O Lord, the floods have lifted up their voice; the floods lift up their waves.

[4] The Lord on high is mightier than the noise of many waters, yea, than the mighty waves of the sea.

[5] Thy testimonies are very sure: holiness becometh thine house, O Lord, for ever.

Psalm 94

O Lord God, to whom vengeance belongeth: O God, to whom vengeance belongeth, shew thyself.

² Lift up thyself, thou judge of the earth: render a reward to the proud.

³ Lord, how long shall the wicked, how long shall the wicked triumph?

⁴ How long shall they utter and speak hard things? and all the workers of iniquity boast themselves?

⁵ They break in pieces thy people, O Lord, and afflict thine heritage.

⁶ They slay the widow and the stranger, and murder the fatherless.

⁷ Yet they say, The Lord shall not see, neither shall the God of Jacob regard it.

⁸ Understand, ye brutish among the people: and ye fools, when will ye be wise?

⁹ He that planteth the ear, shall he not hear? he that formed the eye, shall he not see?

¹⁰ He that chastiseth the heathen, shall not he correct? he that teacheth man knowledge, shall he not know?

¹¹ The Lord knoweth the thoughts of man, that they are but vanity.

¹² Blessed is the man that thou chastenest, O Lord, and teachest him out of thy law;

¹³ That thou mayest give him rest from the days of adversity, until the pit be digged for the wicked.

¹⁴ For the Lord will not cast off his people, neither will he forsake his inheritance.

¹⁵ But judgment shall return unto righteousness: and all the upright in heart shall follow it.

¹⁶ Who will rise up for me against the evildoers? or who will stand up for me against the workers of iniquity?

¹⁷ Unless the Lord had been my help, my soul had almost dwelt in silence.

¹⁸ When I said, My foot slippeth; thy mercy, O Lord, held me up.

¹⁹ In the multitude of my thoughts within me thy comforts delight my soul.

²⁰ Shall the throne of iniquity have fellowship with thee, which frameth mischief by a law?

²¹ They gather themselves together against the soul of the righteous, and condemn the innocent blood.

²² But the Lord is my defence; and my God is the rock of my refuge.

²³ And he shall bring upon them their own iniquity, and shall cut them off in their own wickedness; yea, the Lord our God shall cut them off.

Psalm 95

O come, let us sing unto the Lord: let us make a joyful noise to the rock of our salvation.

² Let us come before his presence with thanksgiving, and make a joyful noise unto him with psalms.

³ For the Lord is a great God, and a great King above all gods.

⁴ In his hand are the deep places of the earth: the strength of the hills is his also.

⁵ The sea is his, and he made it: and his hands formed the dry land.

⁶ O come, let us worship and bow down: let us kneel before the Lord our maker.

⁷ For he is our God; and we are the people of his pasture, and the sheep of his hand. Today if ye will hear his voice,

[8] Harden not your heart, as in the provocation, and as in the day of temptation in the wilderness:

[9] When your fathers tempted me, proved me, and saw my work.

[10] Forty years long was I grieved with this generation, and said, It is a people that do err in their heart, and they have not known my ways:

[11] Unto whom I sware in my wrath that they should not enter into my rest.

Psalm 96

O sing unto the Lord a new song: sing unto the Lord, all the earth.

[2] Sing unto the Lord, bless his name; shew forth his salvation from day to day.

[3] Declare his glory among the heathen, his wonders among all people.

[4] For the Lord is great, and greatly to be praised: he is to be feared above all gods.

[5] For all the gods of the nations are idols: but the Lord made the heavens.

[6] Honour and majesty are before him: strength and beauty are in his sanctuary.

[7] Give unto the Lord, O ye kindreds of the people, give unto the Lord glory and strength.

[8] Give unto the Lord the glory due unto his name: bring an offering, and come into his courts.

[9] O worship the Lord in the beauty of holiness: fear before him, all the earth.

[10] Say among the heathen that the Lord reigneth: the world also shall be established that it shall not be moved: he shall judge the people righteously.

[11] Let the heavens rejoice, and let the earth be glad; let the sea roar, and the fulness thereof.

[12] Let the field be joyful, and all that is therein: then shall all the trees of the wood rejoice

[13] Before the Lord: for he cometh, for he cometh to judge the earth: he shall judge the world with righteousness, and the people with his truth.

Psalm 97

The Lord reigneth; let the earth rejoice; let the multitude of isles be glad thereof.

[2] Clouds and darkness are round about him: righteousness and judgment are the habitation of his throne.

[3] A fire goeth before him, and burneth up his enemies round about.

[4] His lightnings enlightened the world: the earth saw, and trembled.

[5] The hills melted like wax at the presence of the Lord, at the presence of the Lord of the whole earth.

[6] The heavens declare his righteousness, and all the people see his glory.

[7] Confounded be all they that serve graven images, that boast themselves of idols: worship him, all ye gods.

[8] Zion heard, and was glad; and the daughters of Judah rejoiced because of thy judgments, O Lord.

[9] For thou, Lord, art high above all the earth: thou art exalted far above all gods.

[10] Ye that love the Lord, hate evil: he preserveth the souls of his saints; he delivereth them out of the hand of the wicked,

[11] Light is sown for the righteous, and gladness for the upright in heart.

¹² Rejoice in the Lord, ye righeous; and give thanks at the remembrance of his holiness.

Psalm 98

O sing unto the Lord a new song; for he hath done marvellous things: his right hand, and his holy arm, hath gotten him the victory.

² The Lord hath made known his salvation: his righteousness hath he openly shewed in the sight of the heathen.

³ He hath remembered his mercy and his truth toward the house of Israel: all the ends of the earth have seen the salvation of our God.

⁴ Make a joyful noise unto the Lord, all the earth: make a loud noise, and rejoice, and sing praise.

⁵ Sing unto the Lord with the harp; with the harp, and the voice of a psalm.

⁶ With trumpets and sound of cornet make a joyful noise before the Lord, the King.

⁷ Let the sea roar, and the fulness thereof; the world, and they that dwell therein.

⁸ Let the floods clap their hands: let the hills be joyful together

⁹ Before the Lord; for he cometh to judge the earth: with righteousness shall he judge the world, and the people with equity.

Psalm 99

The Lord reigneth: let the people tremble: he sitteth between the cherubims; let the earth be moved.

² The Lord is great in Zion; and he is high above all the people.

³ Let them praise thy great and terrible name; for it is holy.

⁴ The king's strength also loveth judgment; thou dost establish equity, thou executest judgment and righteousness in Jacob.

⁵ Exalt ye the Lord our God, and worship at his footstool; for he is holy.

⁶ Moses and Aaron among his priests, and Samuel among them that call upon his name; they called upon the Lord, and he answered them.

⁷ He spake unto them in the cloudy pillar; they kept his testimonies, and the ordinance that he gave them.

⁸ Thou answeredst them, O Lord our God: thou wast a God that forgavest them, though thou tookest vengeance of their inventions.

⁹ Exalt the Lord our God, and worship at his holy hill; for the Lord our God is holy.

Psalm 100

Make a joyful noise unto the Lord, all ye lands.

² Serve the Lord with gladness: come before his presence with singing.

³ Know ye that the Lord he is God: it is he that hath made us, and not we ourselves; we are his people, and the sheep of his pasture.

⁴ Enter into his gates with thanksgiving, and into his courts with praise: be thankful unto him, and bless his name.

⁵ For the Lord is good; his mercy endureth to all generations.

Psalm 101

I will sing of mercy and iudgment: unto thee, O Lord, will I sing.

² I will behave myself wisely in a perfect way. O when wilt thou come unto me? I will walk within my house with a perfect heart.

³ I will set no wicked thing before mine eyes: I hate the work of them that turn aside; it shall not cleave to me.

⁴ A froward heart shall depart from me: I will not know a wicked person.

⁵ Whoso privily slandereth his neighbour, him will I cut off: him that hath an high look and a proud heart will I not suffer.

⁶ Mine eyes shall be upon the faithful of the land, that they may dwell with me: he that walketh in a perfect way, he shall serve me.

⁷ He that worketh deceit shall not dwell within my house: he that telleth lies shall not tarry in my sight.

⁸ I will early destroy all the wicked of the land; that I may cut off all wicked doers from the city of the Lord.

Psalm 102

Hear my prayer, O Lord, and let my cry come unto thee.

² Hide not thy face from me in the day when I am in trouble; incline thine ear unto me: in the day when I call answer me speedily.

³ For my days are consumed like smoke, and my bones are burned as an hearth.

⁴ My heart is smitten, and withered like grass; so that I forget to eat my bread.

⁵ By reason of the voice of my groaning my bones cleave to my skin.

⁶ I am like a pelican of the wilderness: I am like an owl of the desert.

⁷ I watch, and am as a sparrow alone upon the house top.

⁸ Mine enemies reproach me all the day; and they that are mad against me are sworn against me.

⁹ For I have eaten ashes like bread, and mingled my drink with weeping,

¹⁰ Because of thine indignation and thy wrath: for thou hast lifted me up, and cast me down.

¹¹ My days are like a shadow that declineth; and I am withered like grass.

¹² But thou, O Lord, shalt endure for ever; and thy remembrance unto all generations.

¹³ Thou shalt arise, and have mercy upon Zion: for the time to favour her, yea, the set time, is come.

¹⁴ For thy servants take pleasure in her stones, and favour the dust thereof.

¹⁵ So the heathen shall fear the name of the Lord, and all the kings of the earth thy glory.

¹⁶ When the Lord shall build up Zion, he shall appear in his glory.

¹⁷ He will regard the prayer of the destitute, and not despise their prayer.

¹⁸ This shall be written for the generation to come: and the people which shall be created shall praise the Lord.

¹⁹ For he hath looked down from the height of his sanctuary; from heaven did the Lord behold the earth;

²⁰ To hear the groaning of the prisoner; to loose those that are appointed to death;

²¹ To declare the name of the Lord in Zion, and his praise in Jerusalem;

²² When the people are gathered together, and the kingdoms, to serve the Lord.

²³ He weakened my strength in the way; he shortened my days.

²⁴ I said, O my God, take me not away in the midst of my days; thy years are throughout all generations.

²⁵ Of old hast thou laid the foundation of the earth: and the heavens are the work of thy hands.

²⁶ They shall perish, but thou shalt endure; yea, all of them shall wax old like a garment; as a vesture shalt thou change them, and they shall be changed:

²⁷ But thou art the same, and thy years shall have no end.

²⁸ The children of thy servants shall continue, and their seed shall be established before thee.

Psalm 103

Bless the Lord, O my soul: and all that is within me, bless his holy name.

² Bless the Lord, O my soul, and forget not all his benefits:

³ Who forgiveth all thine iniquities; who healeth all thy diseases;

⁴ Who redeemeth thy life from destruction; who crowneth thee with lovingkindness and tender mercies;

⁵ Who satisfieth thy mouth with good things; so that thy youth is renewed like the eagle's.

⁶ The Lord executeth righteousness and judgment for all that are oppressed.

⁷ He made known his ways unto Moses, his acts unto the children of Israel.

⁸ The Lord is merciful and gracious, slow to anger, and plenteous in mercy.

⁹ He will not always chide: neither will he keep his anger for ever.

¹⁰ He hath not dealt with us after our sins; nor rewarded us according to our iniquities.

¹¹ For as the heaven is high above the earth, so great is his mercy toward them that fear him.

¹² As far as the east is from the west, so far hath he removed our transgressions from us.

¹³ Like as the father pitieth his children, so the Lord pitieth them that fear him.

¹⁴ For he knoweth our frame; he remembereth that we are dust.

¹⁵ As for man, his days are as grass: as a flower of the field, so he flourisheth.

¹⁶ For the wind passeth over it, and it is gone; and the place thereof shall know it no more.

¹⁷ But the mercy of the Lord is from everlasting to everlasting upon them that fear him, and his righteousness unto children's children;

¹⁸ To such as keep his covenant, and to those that remember his commandments to do them.

¹⁹ The Lord hath prepared his throne in the heavens; and his kingdom ruleth over all.

²⁰ Bless the Lord, ye his angels, that excel in strength, that do his commandments, hearkening unto the voice of his word.

²¹ Bless ye the Lord, all ye his hosts; ye ministers of his, that do his pleasure.

²² Bless the Lord, all his works in all places of his dominion; bless the Lord, O my soul.

Psalm 104

Bless the Lord, O my soul. O Lord my God, thou art very great; thou art clothed with honour and majesty.

² Who coverest thyself with light as with a garment: who stretchest out the heavens like a curtain;

³ Who layeth the beams of his chambers in the waters: who maketh the clouds his chariot: who walketh upon the wings of the wind:

⁴ Who maketh his angels spirits: his ministers a flaming fire:

⁵ Who laid the foundations of the earth, that is should not be removed for ever.

⁶ Thou coverest it with the deep as with a garment: the waters stood above the mountains.

⁷ At thy rebuke they fled: at the voice of thy thunder they hasted away.

⁸ They go up by the mountains; they go down by the valleys unto the place which thou hast founded for them.

⁹ Thou hast set a bound that they may not pass over; that they turn not again to cover the earth.

¹⁰ He sendeth the springs into the valleys, which run among the hills.

¹¹ They give drink to every beast of the field: the wild asses quench their thirst.

¹² By them shall the fowls of the heaven have their habitation, which sing among the branches.

¹³ He watereth the hills from his chambers: the earth is satisfied with the fruit of thy works.

¹⁴ He causeth the grass to grow for the cattle, and herb for the service of man: that he may bring forth food out of the earth;

¹⁵ And wine that maketh glad the heart of man, and oil to make his face to shine, and bread which strengtheneth man's heart.

¹⁶ The trees of the Lord are full of sap; the cedars of Lebanon, which he hath planted;

¹⁷ Where the birds make their nests: as for the stork, the fir trees are her house.

¹⁸ The high hills are a refuge for the wild goats; and the rocks for the conies.

¹⁹ He appointed the moon for seasons: the sun knoweth his going down.

²⁰ Thou makest darkness, and it is night: wherein all the beasts of the forest do creep forth.

²¹ The young lions roar after their prey, and seek their meat from God.

²² The sun ariseth, they gather themselves together, and lay them down in their dens.

²³ Man goeth forth unto his work and to his labour until the evening.

²⁴ O Lord, how manifold are thy works! in wisdom hast thou made them all: the earth is full of thy riches.

²⁵ So is this great and wide sea, wherein are things creeping innumerable, both small and great beasts.

²⁶ There go the ships: there is that leviathan, whom thou hast made to play therein.

²⁷ These wait all upon thee; that thou mayest give them their meat in due season.

²⁸ That thou givest them they gather: thou openest thine hand, they are filled with good.

²⁹ Thou hidest thy face, they are troubled: thou takest away their breath, they die, and return to their dust.

³⁰ Thou sendest forth thy spirit, they are created: and thou renewest the face of the earth.

³¹ The glory of the Lord shall endure for ever: the Lord shall rejoice in his works.

³² He looketh on the earth, and it trembleth: he toucheth the hills, and they smoke.

³³ I will sing unto the Lord as long as I live: I will sing praise to my God while I have my being.

³⁴ My meditation of him shall be sweet: I will be glad in the Lord.

³⁵ Let the sinners be consumed out of the earth, and let the wicked be no more. Bless thou the Lord, O my soul. Praise ye the Lord.

Psalm 105

O give thanks unto the Lord; call upon his name: make known his deeds among the people.

² Sing unto him, sing psalms unto him: talk ye of all his wondrous works.

³ Glory ye in his holy name: let the heart of them rejoice that seek the Lord.

⁴ Seek the Lord, and his strength: seek his face evermore.

⁵ Remember his marvellous works that he hath done; his wonders, and the judgments of his mouth;

⁶ O ye seed of Abraham his servant, ye children of Jacob his chosen.

⁷ He is the Lord our God: his judgments are in all the earth.

⁸ He hath remembered his covenant for ever, the word which he commanded to a thousand generations.

⁹ Which covenant he made with Abraham, and his oath unto Isaac;

¹⁰ And confirmed the same unto Jacob for a law, and to Israel for an everlasting covenant:

¹¹ Saying, Unto thee will I give the land of Canaan, the lot of your inheritance:

¹² When they were but a few men in number; yea, very few, and strangers in it.

¹³ When they went from one nation to another, from one kingdom to another people;

¹⁴ He suffered no man to do them wrong: yea, he reproved kings for their sakes;

¹⁵ Saying, Touch not mine anointed, and do my prophets no harm.

¹⁶ Moreover he called for a famine upon the land: he brake the whole staff of bread.

¹⁷ He sent a man before them, even Joseph, who was sold for a servant:

¹⁸ Whose feet they hurt with fetters: he was laid in iron:

¹⁹ Until the time that his word came: the word of the Lord tried him.

²⁰ The king sent and loosed him; even the ruler of the people, and let him go free.

²¹ He made him lord of his house, and ruler of all his substance;

²² To bind his princes at his pleasure; and teach his senators wisdom.

²³ Israel also came into Egypt; and Jacob sojourned in the land of Ham.

²⁴ And he increased his people greatly; and made them stronger than their enemies.

²⁵ He turned their heart to hate his people, to deal subtilly with his servants.

²⁶ He sent Moses his servant; and Aaron whom he had chosen.

²⁷ They shewed his signs among them, and wonders in the land of Ham.

²⁸ He sent darkness, and made it dark; and they rebelled not against his word.

²⁹ He turned their waters into blood, and slew their fish.

³⁰ Their land brought forth frogs in abundance, in the chambers of their kings.

³¹ He spake, and there came divers sorts of flies, and lice in all their coasts.

³² He gave them hail for rain, and flaming fire in their land.

³³ He smote their vines also and their fig trees; and brake the trees of their coasts.

³⁴ He spake, and the locusts came, and caterpillars, and that without number,

³⁵ And did eat up all the herbs in their land, and devoured the fruit of their ground.

³⁶ He smote also all the firstborn in their land, the chief of all their strength.

³⁷ He brought them forth also with silver and gold: and there was not one feeble person among their tribes.

³⁸ Egypt was glad when they departed: for the fear of them fell upon them.

³⁹ He spread a cloud for a covering; and fire to give light in the night.

⁴⁰ The people asked, and he brought quails, and satisfied them with the bread of heaven.

⁴¹ He opened the rock, and the waters gushed out; they ran in the dry places like a river.

⁴² For he remembered his holy promise, and Abraham his servant.

⁴³ And he brought forth his people with joy, and his chosen with gladness:

⁴⁴ And gave them the lands of the heathen: and they inherited the labour of the people;

⁴⁵ That they might observe his statutes, and keep his laws. Praise ye the Lord.

Psalm 106

Praise ye the Lord, O give thanks unto the Lord; for he is good: for his mercy endureth for ever.

² Who can utter the mighty acts of the Lord? who can shew forth all his praise?

³ Blessed are they that keep judgment, and he that doeth right-eousness at all times.

⁴ Remember me, O Lord, with the favour that thou bearest unto thy people: O visit me with thy salvation;

⁵ That I may see the good of thy chosen, that I may rejoice in the gladness of thy nation, that I may glory with thine inheritance.

⁶ We have sinned with our fathers, we have committed iniquity, we have done wickedly.

⁷ Our fathers understood not thy wonders in Egypt; they remem-bered not the multitude of thy mercies; but provoked him at the sea, even at the Red sea.

⁸ Nevertheless he saved them for his name's sake, that he might make his mighty power to be known.

⁹ He rebuked the Red sea also, and it was dried up; so he led them through the depths, as through the wilderness.

¹⁰ And he saved them from the hand of him that hated them, and redeemed them from the hand of the enemy.

¹¹ And the waters covered their enemies: there was not one of them left.

¹² Then believed they his words; they sang his praise.

¹³ They soon forgat his works; they waited not for his counsel:

¹⁴ But lusted exceedingly in the wilderness, and tempted God in the desert.

¹⁵ And he gave them their request; but sent leanness into their soul.

¹⁶ They envied Moses also in the camp, and Aaron the saint of the Lord.

¹⁷ The earth opened and swallowed up Dathan, and covered the company of Abiram.

¹⁸ And a fire was kindled in their company; the flame burned up the wicked.

¹⁹ They made a calf in Horeb, and worshipped the molten image.

²⁰ Thus they changed their glory into the similitude of an ox that eateth grass.

²¹ They forgat God their saviour, which had done great things in Egypt.

²² Wondrous works in the land of Ham, and terrible things by the Red sea.

²³ Therefore he said that he would destroy them, had not Moses his chosen stood before him in the breach, to turn away his wrath, lest he should destroy them.

²⁴ Yea, they despised the pleasant land, they believed not his word:

²⁵ But murmured in their tents, and hearkened not unto the voice of the Lord.

²⁶ Therefore he lifted up his hand against them, to overthrow them in the wilderness:

²⁷ To overthrow their seed also among the nations, and to scatter them in the lands.

²⁸ They joined themselves also unto Baal-peor, and ate the sacrifices of the dead.

²⁹ Thus they provoked him to anger with their inventions: and the plague brake in upon them.

³⁰ Then stood up Phinehas and executed judgment: and so the plague was stayed.

³¹ And that was counted unto him for righteousness unto all generations for evermore.

³² They angered him also at the waters of strife, so that it went ill with Moses for their sakes:

[33] Because they provoked his spirit, so that he spake unadvisedly with his lips.

[34] They did not destoy the nations, concerning whom the Lord commanded them:

[35] But were mingled among the heathen, and learned their words.

[36] And they served their idols: which were a snare unto them.

[37] Yea, they sacrificed their sons and their daughters unto devils,

[38] And shed innocent blood, even the blood of their sons and of their daughters, whom they sacrificed unto the idols of Canaan: and the land was polluted with blood.

[39] Thus were they defiled with their own words, and went a whoring with their own inventions.

[40] Therefore was the wrath of the Lord kindled against his people, insomuch that he abhorred his own inheritance.

[41] And he gave them into the hand of the heathen; and they that hated them ruled over them.

[42] Their enemies also oppressed them, and they were brought into subjection under their hand.

[43] Many times did he deliver them; but they provoked him with their counsel, and were brought low for their iniquity.

[44] Nevertheless he regarded their affliction, when he heard their cry:

[45] And he remembered for them his covenant, and repented according to the multitude of his mercies.

[46] He made them also to be pitied of all those that carried them captives.

[47] Save us, O Lord our God, and gather us from among the heathen, to give thanks unto thy holy name, and to triumph in thy praise.

[48] Blessed be the Lord God of Israel from everlasting to everlasting: and let all the people say, Amen. Praise ye the Lord.

Psalm 107

O give thanks unto the Lord, for his mercy endureth for ever.

[2] Let the redeemed of the Lord say so, whom he hath redeemed from the hand of the enemy;

[3] And gathered them out of the lands, from the east, and from the west, from the north, and from the south.

[4] They wandered in the wilderness in a solitary way; they found no city to dwell in.

[5] Hungry and thirsty, their soul fainted in them.

[6] Then they cried unto the Lord in their trouble, and he delivered them out of their distresses.

[7] And he led them forth by the right way, that they might go to a city of habitation.

[8] Oh that men would praise the Lord for his goodness, and for his wonderful works to the children of men!

[9] For he satisfieth the longing soul, and filleth the hungry soul with goodness.

[10] Such as sit in darkness and in the shadow of death, being bound in affliction and iron;

[11] Because they rebelled against the words of God, and contemned the counsel of the most High:

[12] Therefore he brought down their heart with labour; they fell down, and there was none to help.

[13] Then they cried unto the Lord in their trouble, and he saved them out of their distresses.

[14] He brought them out of darkness and the shadow of death, and brake their bands in sunder.

[15] Oh that men would praise the Lord for his goodness, and for his wonderful works to the children of men!

¹⁶ For he hath broken the gates of brass, and cut the bars of iron in sunder.

¹⁷ Fools because of their transgression, and because of their iniquities, are afflicted.

¹⁸ Their soul abhorreth all manner of meat; and they draw near unto the gates of death.

¹⁹ Then they cry unto the Lord in their trouble, and he saveth them out of their distresses.

²⁰ He sent his word, and healed them, and delivered them from their destructions.

²¹ O that men would praise the Lord for his goodness, and for his wonderful works to the children of men!

²² And let them sacrifice the sacrifices of thanksgiving, and declare his works with rejoicing.

²³ They that go down to the sea in ships, that do business in great waters;

²⁴ These see the works of the Lord, and his wonders in the deep.

²⁵ For he commandeth, and raiseth the stormy wind, which lifteth up the waves thereof.

²⁶ They mount up to the heaven, they go down again to the depths: their soul is melted because of trouble.

²⁷ They reel to and fro, and stagger like a drunken man, and are at their wit's end.

²⁸ Then they cry unto the Lord in their trouble, and he bringeth them out of their distresses.

²⁹ He maketh the storm a calm, so that the waves thereof are still.

³⁰ Then are they glad because they be quiet; so he bringeth them unto their desired haven.

³¹ Oh that men would praise the Lord for his goodness, and for his wonderful works to the children of men!

³² Let them exalt him also in the congregation of the people, and praise him in the assembly of the elders.

³³ He turneth rivers into a wilderness, and the watersprings into dry ground;

³⁴ A fruitful land into barrenness, for the wickedness of them that dwell therein.

³⁵ He turneth the wilderness into a standing water, and dry gound into watersprings.

³⁶ And there he maketh the hungry to dwell, that they may prepare a city for habitation;

³⁷ And sow the fields, and plant vineyards, which may yield fruits of increase.

³⁸ He blesseth them also, so that they are multiplied greatly; and suffereth not their cattle to decrease.

³⁹ Again, they are minished and brought low through oppression, affliction, and sorrow.

⁴⁰ He poureth contempt upon princes, and causeth them to wander in the wilderness, where there is no way.

⁴¹ Yet setteth he the poor on high from affliction, and maketh him families like a flock.

⁴² The righteous shall see it and reioice: and all iniquity shall stop her mouth.

⁴³ Whoso is wise, and will observe these things, even they shall understand the lovingkindness of the Lord.

Psalm 108

O God, my heart is fixed; I will sing and give praise, even with my glory.

² Awake, psaltery and harp: I myself will awake early.

³ I will praise thee, O Lord, among the people: and I will sing praises unto thee among the nations.

⁴ For thy mercy is great above the heavens: and thy truth reacheth unto the clouds.

⁵ Be thou exalted, O God, above the heavens: and thy glory above all the earth;

⁶ That thy beloved may be delivered: save with thy right hand, and answer me.

⁷ God hath spoken in his holiness; I will rejoice, I will divide Shechem, and mete out the valley of Succoth.

⁸ Gilead is mine; Manasseh is mine; Ephraim also is the strength of mine head; Judah is my lawgiver;

⁹ Moab is my washpot; over Edom will I cast out my shoe; over Philistia will I triumph.

¹⁰ Who will bring me into the strong city? who will lead me into Edom?

¹¹ Wilt not thou, O God, who hast cast us off? and wilt not thou, O God, go forth with our hosts?

¹² Give us help from trouble: for vain is the help of man.

¹³ Through God we shall do valiantly: for he it is that shall tread down our enemies.

Psalm 109

Hold not thy peace, O God of my praise;

² For the mouth of the wicked and the mouth of the deceitful are opened against me: they have spoken against me with a lying tongue.

[3] They compassed me about also with words of hatred; and fought against me without a cause.

[4] For my love they are my adversaries: but I give myself unto prayer.

[5] And they have rewarded me evil for good, and hatred for my love.

[6] Set thou a wicked man over him: and let Satan stand at his right hand.

[7] When he shall be judged, let him be condemned: and let his prayer become sin.

[8] Let his days be few; and let another take his office.

[9] Let his children be fatherless, and his wife a widow.

[10] Let his children be continually vagabonds, and beg: let them seek their bread also out of their desolate places.

[11] Let the extortioner catch all that he hath; and let the strangers spoil his labour.

[12] Let there be none to extend mercy unto him: neither let there be any to favour his fatherless children.

[13] Let his posterity be cut off; and in the generation following let their name be blotted out.

[14] Let the iniquity of his fathers be remembered with the Lord; and let not the sin of his mother be blotted out.

[15] Let them be before the Lord continually, that he may cut off the memory of them from the earth.

[16] Because that he remembered not to shew mercy, but persecuted the poor and needy man, that he might even slay the broken in heart.

[17] As he loved cursing, so let it come unto him: as he delighted not in blessing, so let it be far from him.

¹⁸ As he clothed himself with cursing like as with his garment, so let it come into his bowels like water, and like oil into his bones.

¹⁹ Let it be unto him as the garment which covereth him, and for a girdle wherewith he is girded continually.

²⁰ Let this be the reward of mine adversaries from the Lord, and of them that speak evil against my soul.

²¹ But do thou for me, O God the Lord, for thy name's sake: because thy mercy is good, deliver thou me.

²² For I am poor and needy, and my heart is wounded within me.

²³ I am gone like the shadow when it declineth: I am tossed up and down as the locust.

²⁴ My knees are weak through fasting; and my flesh faileth of fatness.

²⁵ I became also a reproach unto them, when they looked upon me they shaked their heads.

²⁶ Help me, O Lord my God: O save me according to thy mercy:

²⁷ That they may know that this is thy hand; that thou, Lord, hast done it.

²⁸ Let them curse, but bless thou: when they arise, let them be ashamed; but let thy servant rejoice.

²⁹ Let mine adversaries be clothed with shame, and let them cover themselves with their own confusion, as with a mantle.

³⁰ I will greatly praise the Lord with my mouth; yea, I will praise him among the multitude.

³¹ For he shall stand at the right hand of the poor, to save him from those that condemn his soul.

Psalm 110

The Lord said unto my Lord, Sit thou at my right hand, until I make thine enemies thy footstool.

² The Lord shall send the rod of thy strength out of Zion: rule thou in the midst of thine enemies.

³ Thy people shall be willing in the day of thy power, in the beauties of holiness from the womb of the morning: thou hast the dew of thy youth.

⁴ The Lord hath sworn, and will not repent, Thou art a priest for ever after the order of Melchizedek.

⁵ The Lord at thy right hand shall strike through kings in the day of his wrath.

⁶ He shall judge among the heathen, he shall fill the places with the dead bodies; he shall wound the heads over many countries.

⁷ He shall drink of the brook in the way: therefore shall he lift up the head.

Psalm 111

Praise ye the Lord. I will praise the Lord with my whole heart, in the assembly of the upright, and in the congregation.

² The works of the Lord are great, sought out of all them that have pleasure therein.

³ His work is honourable and glorious: and his righteousness endureth for ever.

⁴ He hath made his wonderful works to be remembered: the Lord is gracious and full of compassion.

⁵ He hath given meat unto them that fear him: he will ever be mindful of his convenant.

⁶ He hath shewed his people the power of his works, that he may give them the heritage of the heathen.

⁷ The works of his hands are verity and judgment; all his commandments are sure.

[8] They stand fast for ever and ever, and are done in truth and uprightness.

[9] He sent redemption unto his people: he hath commanded his covenant for ever: holy and reverend is his name.

[10] The fear of the Lord is the beginning of wisdom: a good understanding have all they that do his commandments: his praise endureth for ever.

Psalm 112

Praise ye the Lord. Blessed is the man that feareth the Lord, that delighteth greatly in his commandments.

[2] His seed shall be mighty upon earth: the generation of the upright shall be blessed.

[3] Wealth and riches shall be in his house: and his righteousness endureth for ever.

[4] Unto the upright there ariseth light in the darkness: he is gracious, and full of compassion, and righteous.

[5] A good man sheweth favour, and lendeth; he will guide his affairs with discretion.

[6] Surely he shall not be moved for ever: the righteous shall be in everlasting remembrance.

[7] He shall not be afraid of evil tidings: his heart is fixed, trusting in the Lord.

[8] His heart is established, he shall not be afraid, until he see his desire upon his enemies.

[9] He hath dispersed, he hath given to the poor; his righteousness endureth for ever; his horn shall be exalted with honour.

[10] The wicked shall see it, and be grieved; he shall gnash with his teeth, and melt away: the desire of the wicked shall perish.

Psalm 113

Praise ye the Lord. Praise, O ye servants of the Lord, praise the name of the Lord.

² Blessed be the name of the Lord from this time forth and for evermore.

³ From the rising of the sun unto the going down of the same the Lord's name is to be praised.

⁴ The Lord is high above all nations, and his glory above the heavens.

⁵ Who is like unto the Lord our God, who dwelleth on high,

⁶ Who humbleth himself to behold the things that are in heaven, and in the earth!

⁷ He raiseth up the poor out of the dust, and lifteth the needy out of the dunghill;

⁸ That he may set him with princes, even with the princes of his people.

⁹ He maketh the barren woman to keep house, and to be a joyful mother of children. Praise ye the Lord.

Psalm 114

When Israel went out of Egypt, the house of Jacob from a people of strange language;

² Judah was his sanctuary, and Israel his dominion.

³ The sea saw it and fled: Jordan was driven back.

⁴ The mountains skipped like rams, and the little hills like lambs.

⁵ What ailed thee, O thou sea, that thou fleddest? thou Jordan, that thou wast driven back?

⁶ Ye mountains, that ye skipped like rams; and ye little hills, like lambs?

⁷ Tremble, thou earth, at the presence of the Lord, at the presence of the God of Jacob;

⁸ Which turned the rock into a standing water, the flint into a fountain of waters.

Psalm 115

Not unto us, O Lord, not unto us, but unto thy name give glory, for thy mercy, and for thy truth's sake.

² Wherefore should the heathen say, Where is now their God?

³ But our God is in the heavens: he hath done whatsoever he hath pleased.

⁴ Their idols are silver and gold, the work of men's hands.

⁵ They have mouths, but they speak not: eyes have they, but they see not:

⁶ They have ears, but they hear not: noses have they, but they smell not:

⁷ They have hands, but they handle not: feet have they, but they walk not: neither speak they through their throat.

⁸ They that make them are like unto them; so is every one that trusteth in them.

⁹ O Israel, trust thou in the Lord: he is their help and their shield.

¹⁰ O house of Aaron, trust in the Lord: he is their help and their shield.

¹¹ Ye that fear the Lord, trust in the Lord: he is their help and their shield.

¹² The Lord hath been mindful of us: he will bless us; he will bless the house of Israel; he will bless the house of Aaron.

¹³ He will bless them that fear the Lord, both small and great.

¹⁴ The Lord shall increase you more and more, you and your children.

¹⁵ Ye are blessed of the Lord which made heaven and earth.

¹⁶ The heaven, even the heavens, are the Lord's: but the earth hath he given to the children of men.

¹⁷ The dead praise not the Lord, neither any that go down in silence.

¹⁸ But we will bless the Lord from this time forth and for evermore. Praise the Lord.

Psalm 116

I love the Lord, because he hath heard my voice and my supplications.

² Because he hath inclined his ear unto me, therefore will I call upon him as long as I live.

³ The sorrows of death compassed me, and the pains of hell gat hold upon me: I found trouble and sorrow.

⁴ Then called I upon the name of the Lord; O Lord, I beseech thee, deliver my soul.

⁵ Gracious is the Lord, and righteous; yea, our God is merciful.

⁶ The Lord preserveth the simple: I was brought low and he helped me.

⁷ Return unto thy rest, O my soul; for the Lord hath dealt bountifully with thee.

⁸ For thou hast delivered my soul from death, mine eyes from tears, and my feet from falling.

⁹ I will walk before the Lord in the land of the living.

¹⁰ I believed, therefore have I spoken: I was greatly afflicted;

¹¹ I said in my haste, All men are liars.

¹² What shall I render unto the Lord for all his benefits toward me?

¹³ I will take the cup of salvation, and call upon the name of the Lord.

¹⁴ I will pay my vows unto the Lord now in the presence of all his people.

¹⁵ Precious in the sight of the Lord is the death of his saints.

¹⁶ O Lord, truly I am thy servant; I am thy servant, and the son of thine handmaid: thou hast loosed my bonds.

¹⁷ I will offer to thee the sacrifice of thanksgiving, and will call upon the name of the Lord,

¹⁸ I will pay my vows unto the Lord now in the presence of all his people.

¹⁹ In the courts of the Lord's house, in the midst of thee, O Jerusalem. Praise ye the Lord.

Psalm 117

O praise the Lord, all ye nations: praise him, all ye people.

² For his merciful kindness is great toward us: and the truth of the Lord endureth for ever. Praise ye the Lord.

Psalm 118

O give thanks unto the Lord; for he is good: because his mercy endureth for ever.

² Let Israel now say, that his mercy endureth for ever.

³ Let the house of Aaron now say, that his mercy endureth for ever.

⁴ Let them now that fear the Lord say, that his mercy endureth for ever.

⁵ I called upon the Lord in distress: the Lord answered me, and set me in a large place.

[6] The Lord is on my side; I will not fear: what can man do unto me?

[7] The Lord taketh my part with them that help me: therefore shall I see my desire upon them that hate me.

[8] It is better to trust in the Lord than to put confidence in man.

[9] It is better to trust in the Lord than to put confidence in princes.

[10] All nations compassed me about: but in the name of the Lord will I destroy them.

[11] They compassed me about; yea, they compassed me about: but in the name of the Lord I will destroy them.

[12] They compassed me about like bees; they are quenched as the fire of thorns: for in the name of the Lord I will destroy them.

[13] Thou hast thrust sore at me that I might fall: but the Lord helped me.

[14] The Lord is my strength and song, and is become my salvation.

[15] The voice of rejoicing and salvation is in the tabernacles of the righteous: the right hand of the Lord doeth valiantly.

[16] The right hand of the Lord is exalted: the right hand of the Lord doeth valiantly.

[17] I shall not die, but live, and declare the works of the Lord.

[18] The Lord hath chastened me sore: but he hath not given me over unto death.

[19] Open to me the gates of righteousness: I will go into them, and I will praise the Lord:

[20] This gate of the Lord, into which the righteous shall enter.

[21] I will praise thee: for thou hast heard me, and art become my salvation.

²² The stone which the builders refused is become the head stone of the corner.

²³ This is the Lord's doing; it is marvellous in our eyes.

²⁴ This is the day which the Lord hath made; we will rejoice and be glad in it,

²⁵ Save now, I beseech thee, O Lord: O Lord, I beseech thee, send now prosperity,

²⁶ Blessed be he that cometh in the name of the Lord: we have blessed you out of the house of the Lord.

²⁷ God is the Lord, which hath shewed us light: bind the sacrifice with cords, even unto the horns of the altar.

²⁸ Thou art my God, and I will praise thee: thou art my God, I will exalt thee.

²⁹ O give thanks unto the Lord; for he is good: for his mercy endureth for ever.

Psalm 119

Blessed are the undefiled in the way, who walk in the law of the Lord.

² Blessed are they that keep his testimonies, and that seek him with the whole heart.

³ They also do no iniquity: they walk in his ways.

⁴ Thou hast commanded us to keep thy precepts diligently.

⁵ O that my ways were directed to keep thy statutes!

⁶ Then shall I not be ashamed, when I have respect unto all thy commandments.

⁷ I will praise thee with uprightness of heart, when I shall have learned thy righteous judgments.

⁸ I will keep thy statutes: O forsake me not utterly.

[9] Wherewithal shall a young man cleanse his way? by taking heed thereto according to thy word.

[10] With my whole heart have I sought thee; O let me not wander from thy commandments.

[11] Thy word have I hid in mine heart, that I might not sin against thee.

[12] Blessed art thou, O Lord: teach me thy statutes.

[13] With my lips have I declared all the judgments of thy mouth.

[14] I have rejoiced in the way of thy testimonies, as much as in all riches.

[15] I will meditate in thy precepts, and have respect unto thy ways.

[16] I will delight myself in thy statutes: I will not forget thy word.

[17] Deal bountifully with thy servant, that I may live, and keep thy word.

[18] Open thou mine eyes, that I may behold wondrous things out of thy law.

[19] I am a stranger in the earth: hide not thy commandments from me.

[20] My soul breaketh for the longing that it hath unto thy judgments at all times.

[21] Thou hast rebuked the proud that are cursed, which do err from thy commandments.

[22] Remove from me reproach and contempt; for I have kept thy testimonies.

[23] Princes also did sit and speak against me: but thy servant did meditate in thy statutes.

[24] Thy testimonies also are my delight and my counsellors.

²⁵ My soul cleaveth unto the dust: quicken thou me according to thy word.

²⁶ I have declared thy ways, and thou heardest me: teach me thy statutes.

²⁷ Make me to understand the way of thy precepts: so shall I talk of thy wondrous works.

²⁸ My soul melteth for heaviness: strengthen thou me according unto thy word.

²⁹ Remove from me the way of lying: and grant me thy law graciously.

³⁰ I have chosen the way of truth: thy judgments have I laid before me.

³¹ I have stuck unto thy testimonies: O Lord, put me not to shame.

³² I will run the way of thy commandments, when thou shalt enlarge my heart.

³³ Teach me, O Lord, the way of thy statutes; and I shall keep it unto the end.

³⁴ Give me understanding, and I shall keep thy law; yea, I shall observe it with my whole heart.

³⁵ Make me to go in the path of thy commandments; for therein do I delight.

³⁶ Incline my heart unto thy testimonies, and not to covetousness.

³⁷ Turn away mine eyes from beholding vanity; and quicken thou me in thy way.

³⁸ Stablish thy word unto thy servant, who is devoted to thy fear.

³⁹ Turn away my reproach which I fear: for thy judgments are good.

⁴⁰ Behold, I have longed after thy precepts: quicken me in thy righteousness.

⁴¹ Let thy mercies come also unto me, O Lord, even thy salvation, according to thy word.

⁴² So shall I have wherewith to answer him that reproacheth me: for I trust in thy word.

⁴³ And take not the word of truth utterly out of my mouth; for I have hoped in thy judgments.

⁴⁴ So shall I keep thy law continually for ever and ever.

⁴⁵ And I will walk at liberty: for I seek thy precepts.

⁴⁶ I will speak of thy testimonies also before kings, and will not be ashamed.

⁴⁷ And I will delight myself in thy commandments, which I have loved.

⁴⁸ My hands also will I lift up unto thy commandments, which I have loved; and I will meditate in thy statutes.

⁴⁹ Remember the word unto thy servant, upon which thou hast caused me to hope.

⁵⁰ This is my comfort in my affliction: for thy word hath quickened me.

⁵¹ The proud have had me greatly in derision: yet have I not declined from thy law.

⁵² I remembered thy judgments of old, O Lord; and have comforted myself.

⁵³ Horror hath taken hold upon me because of the wicked that forsake thy law.

⁵⁴ Thy statutes have been my songs in the house of my pilgrimage.

⁵⁵ I have remembered thy name, O Lord, in the night, and have kept thy law.

⁵⁶ This I had, because I kept thy precepts.

⁵⁷ Thou art my portion, O Lord: I have said that I would keep thy words.

⁵⁸ I intreated thy favour with my whole heart: be merciful unto me according to thy word.

⁵⁹ I thought on my ways, and turned my feet unto thy testimonies.

⁶⁰ I made haste, and delayed not to keep thy commandments.

⁶¹ The bands of the wicked have robbed me: but I have not forgotten thy law.

⁶² At midnight I will rise to give thanks unto thee because of thy righteous judgments.

⁶³ I am a companion of all them that fear thee, and of them that keep thy precepts.

⁶⁴ The earth, O Lord, is full of thy mercy: teach me thy statutes.

⁶⁵ Thou hast dwelt well with thy servant, O Lord, according to thy word.

⁶⁶ Teach me good judgment and knowledge: for I have believed thy commandments.

⁶⁷ Before I was afflicted I went astray: but now I have kept thy word.

⁶⁸ Thou art good, and doest good; teach me thy statutes.

⁶⁹ The proud have forged a lie against me: but I will keep thy precepts with my whole heart.

⁷⁰ Their heart is as fat as grease; but I delight in thy law.

⁷¹ It is good for me that I have been afflicted; that I might learn thy statutes.

⁷² The law of thy mouth is better unto me than thousands of gold and silver.

⁷³ Thy hands have made me and fashioned me: give me understanding, that I may learn thy commandments.

[74] They that fear thee will be glad when they see me; because I have hoped in thy word.

[75] I know, O Lord, that thy judgments are right, and that thou in faithfulness hast afflicted me.

[76] Let, I pray thee, thy merciful kindness be for my comfort, according to thy word unto thy servant.

[77] Let thy tender mercies come unto me, that I may live: for thy law is my delight.

[78] Let the proud be ashamed; for they dealt perversely with me without a cause: but I will meditate in thy precepts.

[79] Let those that fear thee turn unto me, and those that have known thy testimonies.

[80] Let my heart be sound in thy statutes; that I be not ashamed.

[81] My soul fainteth for thy salvation: but I hope in thy word.

[82] Mine eyes fail for thy word, saying, When wilt thou comfort me?

[83] For I am become like a bottle in the smoke; yet do I not forget thy statutes.

[84] How many are the days of thy servant? when wilt thou execute judgment on them that persecute me?

[85] The proud have digged pits for me, which are not after thy law.

[86] All thy commandments are faithful: they persecute me wrongfully; help thou me.

[87] They had almost consumed me upon earth; but I forsook not thy precepts.

[88] Quicken me after thy lovingkindness; so shall I keep the testimony of thy mouth.

[89] For ever, O Lord, thy word is settled in heaven.

⁹⁰ Thy faithfulness is unto all generations: thou hast established the earth, and it abideth.

⁹¹ They continue this day according to thine ordinances: for all are thy servants.

⁹² Unless thy law had been my delights, I should then have perished in mine affliction.

⁹³ I will never forget thy precepts: for with them thou hast quickened me.

⁹⁴ I am thine, save me; for I have sought thy precepts.

⁹⁵ The wicked have waited for me to destroy me: but I will consider thy testimonies.

⁹⁶ I have seen an end of all perfection: but thy commandment is exceeding broad.

⁹⁷ O how I love thy law! it is my meditation all the day.

⁹⁸ Thou through thy commandments hast made me wiser than mine enemies: for they are ever with me.

⁹⁹ I have more understanding than all my teachers: for thy testimonies are my meditation.

¹⁰⁰ I understand more than the ancients, because I keep thy precepts.

¹⁰¹ I have refrained my feet from every evil way, that I might keep thy word.

¹⁰² I have not departed from thy judgments: for thou hast taught me.

¹⁰³ How sweet are thy words unto my taste! yea, sweeter than honey to my mouth!

¹⁰⁴ Through thy precepts I get understanding: therefore I hate every false way.

¹⁰⁵ Thy word is a lamp unto my feet, and a light unto my path.

¹⁰⁶ I have sworn, and I will perform it, that I will keep thy righteous judgments.

¹⁰⁷ I am afflicted very much: quicken me, O Lord, according unto thy word.

¹⁰⁸ Accept, I beseech thee, the freewill offerings of my mouth, O Lord, and teach me thy judgments.

¹⁰⁹ My soul is continually in my hand: yet do I not forget thy law.

¹¹⁰ The wicked have laid a snare for me: yet I erred not from thy precepts.

¹¹¹ Thy testimonies have I taken as an heritage for ever: for they are the rejoicing of my heart.

¹¹² I have inclined mine heart to perform thy statutes alway, even unto the end.

¹¹³ I hate vain thoughts: but thy law do I love.

¹¹⁴ Thou art my hiding place and my shield: I hope in thy word.

¹¹⁵ Depart from me, ye evildoers: for I will keep the commandments of my God.

¹¹⁶ Uphold me according unto thy word, that I may live: and let me not be ashamed of my hope.

¹¹⁷ Hold thou me up, and I shall be safe: and I will have respect unto thy statutes continually.

¹¹⁸ Thou hast trodden down all them that err from thy statutes: for their deceit is falsehood.

¹¹⁹ Thou puttest away all the wicked of the earth like dress: therefore I love thy testimonies.

¹²⁰ My flesh trembleth for fear of thee; and I am afraid of thy judgments.

[121] I have done judgment and justice: leave me not to mine oppressors.

[122] Be surety for thy servant for good: let not the proud oppress me.

[123] Mine eyes fail for thy salvation, and for the word of thy righteousness.

[124] Deal with thy servant according unto thy mercy, and teach me thy statutes.

[125] I am thy servant; give me understanding, that I may know thy testimonies.

[126] It is time for thee, Lord, to work: for they have made void thy law.

[127] Therefore I love thy commandments above gold: yea, above fine gold.

[128] Therefore I esteem all thy precepts concerning all things to be right; and I hate every false way.

[129] Thy testimonies are wonderful: therefore doth my soul keep them.

[130] The entrance of thy words giveth light; it giveth understanding unto the simple.

[131] I opened my mouth, and panted: for I longed for thy commandments.

[132] Look thou upon me, and be merciful unto me, as thou usest to do unto those that love thy name.

[133] Order my steps in thy word: and let not any iniquity have dominion over me.

[134] Deliver me from the oppression of man: so will I keep thy precepts.

[135] Make thy face to shine upon thy servant; and teach me thy statutes.

¹³⁶ Rivers of water run down mine eyes, because they keep not thy law.

¹³⁷ Righteous art thou, O Lord, and upright are thy judgments.

¹³⁸ Thy testimonies that thou hast commanded are righteous and very faithful.

¹³⁹ My zeal hath consumed me, because mine enemies have forgotten thy words.

¹⁴⁰ Thy word is very pure: therefore thy servant loveth it.

¹⁴¹ I am small and despised: yet do not I forget thy precepts.

¹⁴² Thy righteousness is an everlasting righteousness, and thy law is the truth.

¹⁴³ Trouble and anguish have taken hold on me: yet thy commandments are my delights.

¹⁴⁴ The righteousness of thy testimonies is everlasting: give me understanding, and I shall live.

¹⁴⁵ I cried with my whole heart; hear me, O Lord: I will keep thy statutes.

¹⁴⁶ I cried unto thee; save me, and I shall keep thy testimonies.

¹⁴⁷ I prevented the dawning of the morning, and cried: I hoped in thy word.

¹⁴⁸ Mine eyes prevent the night watches, that I might meditate in thy word.

¹⁴⁹ Hear my voice according unto thy lovingkindness: O Lord, quicken me according to thy judgment.

¹⁵⁰ They draw nigh that follow after mischief: they are far from thy law.

¹⁵¹ Thou art near, O Lord; and all thy commandments are truth.

[152] Concerning thy testimonies, I have known of old that thou hast founded them for ever.

[153] Consider mine affliction, and deliver me: for I do not forget thy law.

[154] Plead my cause, and deliver me: quicken me according to thy word.

[155] Salvation is far from the wicked: for they seek not thy statutes.

[156] Great are thy tender mercies, O Lord: quicken me according to thy judgments.

[157] Many are my persecutors and mine enemies; yet do I not decline from thy testimonies.

[158] I beheld the transgressors, and was grieved; because they kept not thy word.

[159] Consider how I love thy precepts: quicken me, O Lord, according to thy lovingkindness.

[160] Thy word is true from the beginning: and every one of thy righteous judgments endureth for ever.

[161] Princes have persecuted me without a cause: but my heart standeth in awe of thy word.

[162] I rejoice at thy word, as one that findeth great spoil.

[163] I hate and abhor lying: but thy law do I love.

[164] Seven times a day do I praise thee because of thy righteous judgments.

[165] Great peace have they which love thy law: and nothing shall offend them.

[166] Lord, I have hoped for thy salvation, and done thy commandments.

[167] My soul hath kept thy testimonies; and I love them exceedingly.

[168] I have kept thy precepts and thy testimonies: for all my ways are before thee.

[169] Let my cry come near before thee, O Lord: give me understanding according to thy word.

[170] Let my supplication come before thee: deliver according to thy word.

[171] My lips shall utter praise, when thou hast taught me thy statutes.

[172] My tongue shall speak of thy word: for all thy commandments are righteousness.

[173] Let thine hand help me; for I have chosen thy precepts.

[174] I have longed for thy salvation, O Lord; and thy law is my delight.

[175] Let my soul live, and it shall praise thee; and let thy judgments help me.

[176] I have gone astray like a lost sheep; seek thy servant; for I do not forget thy commandments.

Psalm 120

In my distress I cried unto the Lord, and he heard me.

[2] Deliver my soul, O Lord, from lying lips, and from a deceitful tongue,

[3] What shall be given unto thee? or what shall be done unto thee, thou false tongue?

[4] Sharp arrows of the mighty, with coals of juniper.

[5] Woe is me, that I sojourn in Mesech, that I dwell in the tents of Kedar!

[6] My soul hath long dwelt with him that hateth peace.

[7] I am for peace: but when I speak, they are for war.

Psalm 121

I will lift up mine eyes unto the hills, from whence cometh my help.

² My help cometh from the Lord, which made heaven and earth.

³ He will not suffer thy foot to be moved; he that keepeth thee will not slumber.

⁴ Behold, he that keepeth Israel shall neither slumber nor sleep.

⁵ The Lord is thy keeper: the Lord is thy shade upon thy right hand.

⁶ The sun shall not smite thee by day, nor the moon by night.

⁷ The Lord shall preserve thee from all evil: he shall preserve thy soul.

⁸ The Lord shall preserve thy going out and thy coming in from this time forth, and even for evermore.

Psalm 122

I was glad when thy said unto me, Let us go into the house of the Lord.

² Our feet shall stand within thy gates, O Jerusalem.

³ Jerusalem is builded as a city that is compact together.

⁴ Whither the tribes go up, the tribes of the Lord, unto the testimony of Israel, to give thanks unto the name of the Lord.

⁵ For there are set thrones of judgment, the thrones of the house of David.

⁶ Pray for the peace of Jerusalem: they shall prosper that love thee.

⁷ Peace be within thy walls, and prosperity within thy palaces.

⁸ For my brethren and companions' sakes, I will not say, Peace be within thee.

⁹ Because of the house of the Lord our God I will seek thy good.

Psalm 123

Unto thee lift I up mine eyes, O thou that dwellest in the heavens.

² Behold, as the eyes of servants look unto the hand of their masters, and as the eyes of a maiden unto the hand of her mistress; so our eyes wait upon the Lord our God, until that he have mercy upon us.

³ Have mercy upon us, O Lord, have mercy upon us: for we are exceedingly filled with contempt.

⁴ Our soul is exceedingly filled with the scorning of those that are at ease, and with the contempt of the proud.

Psalm 124

If it had not been the Lord who was on our side, now may Israel say:

² If it had not been the Lord who was on our side, when men rose up against us:

³ Then they had swallowed us up quick, when their wrath was kindled against us:

⁴ Then the waters had overwhelmed us, the stream had gone over our soul:

⁵ Then the proud waters had gone over our soul.

⁶ Blessed be the Lord, who hath not given us as a prey to their teeth.

⁷ Our soul is escaped as a bird out of the snare of the fowlers: the snare is broken, and we are escaped.

⁸ Our help is in the name of the Lord, who made heaven and earth.

Psalm 125

They that trust in the Lord shall be as mount Zion, which cannot be removed, but abideth for ever.

² As the mountains are round about Jerusalem, so the Lord is round about his people from henceforth even for ever.

³ For the rod of the wicked shall not rest upon the lot of the righteous; lest the righteous put forth their hands unto iniquity.

⁴ Do good, O Lord, unto those that be good, and to them that are upright in their hearts.

⁵ As for such as turn aside unto their crooked ways, the Lord shall lead them forth with the workers of iniquity: but peace shall be upon Israel.

Psalm 126

When the Lord turned again the captivity of Zion, we were like them that dream.

² Then was our mouth filled with laughter, and our tongue with singing: then said they among the heathen, The Lord hath done great things for them.

³ The Lord hath done great things for us; whereof we are glad.

⁴ Turn again our captivity, O Lord, as the streams in the south.

⁵ They that sow in tears shall reap in joy.

⁶ He that goeth forth and weepeth, bearing precious seed, shall doubtless come again with rejoicing, bringing his sheaves with him.

Psalm 127

Except the Lord build the house, they labour in vain that build it: except the Lord keep the city, the watchman waketh but in vain.

² It is vain for you to rise up early, to sit up late, to eat the bread of sorrows: for so he giveth his beloved sleep.

³ Lo, children are an heritage of the Lord: and the fruit of the womb is his reward.

⁴ As arrows are in the hand of a mighty man; so are the children of the youth.

⁵ Happy is the man that hath his quiver full of them: they shall not be ashamed, but they shall speak with the enemies in the gate.

Psalm 128

Blessed is every one that feareth the Lord; that walketh in his ways.

² For thou shalt eat the labour of thine hands: happy shalt thou be, and it shall be well with thee.

³ Thy wife shall be as a fruitful vine by the sides of thine house: thy children like olive plants round about thy table.

⁴ Behold, that thus shall the man be blessed that feareth the Lord.

⁵ The Lord shall bless thee out of Zion: and thou shalt see the good of Jerusalem all the days of thy life.

⁶ Yea, thou shalt see thy children's children, and peace upon Israel.

Psalm 129

Many a time have they afflicted me from my youth, may Israel now say:

² Many a time have they afflicted me from youth: yet they have not prevailed against me.

³ The plowers plowed upon my back: they made long their furrows.

⁴ The Lord is righteous: he hath cut asunder the cords of the wicked.

⁵ Let them all be confounded and turned back that hate Zion.

⁶ Let them be as the grass upon the housetops, which withereth afore it groweth up.

⁷ Wherewith the mower filleth not his hand; nor he that bindeth sheaves his bosom.

⁸ Neither do they which go by say, The blessing of the Lord be upon you: we bless you in the name of the Lord.

Psalm 130

Out of the depths have I cried unto thee, O Lord.

² Lord, hear my voice: let thine ears be attentive to the voice of my supplications.

³ If thou, Lord, shouldest mark iniquities, O Lord, who shall stand?

⁴ But there is forgiveness with thee, that thou mayest be feared.

⁵ I wait for the Lord, my soul doth wait, and in his word do I hope.

⁶ My soul waiteth for the Lord more than they that watch for the morning: I say, more than they that watch for the morning.

⁷ Let Israel hope in the Lord: for with the Lord there is mercy, and with him is plenteous redemption.

⁸ And he shall redeem Israel from all his iniquities.

Psalm 131

Lord, my heart is not haughty, nor mine eyes lofty: neither do I exercise myself in great matters, or in things too high for me.

² Surely I have behaved and quieted myself, as a child that is weaned of his mother: my soul is even as a weaned child.

³ Let Israel hope in the Lord from henceforth and for ever.

Psalm 132

Lord, remember David, and all his afflictions:

² How he sware unto the Lord, and vowed the mighty God of Jacob;

³ Surely I will not come into the tabernacle of my house, nor go up into my bed;

⁴ I will not give sleep to mine eyes, or slumber to mine eyelids.

⁵ Until I find out a place for the Lord, an habitation for the mighty God of Jacob.

⁶ Lo, we heard of it at Ephratah: we found it in the fields of the wood.

⁷ We will go into his tabernacles: we will worship at his footstool.

⁸ Arise, O Lord, into thy rest; thou, and the ark of thy strength.

⁹ Let thy priests be clothed with righteousness; and let thy saints shout for joy.

¹⁰ For thy servant David's sake turn not away the face of thine anointed.

¹¹ The Lord hath sworn in truth unto David; he will not turn from it; Of the fruit of thy body will I set upon thy throne.

¹² If thy children will keep my covenant and my testimony that I shall teach them, their children shall also sit upon thy throne for evermore.

¹³ For the Lord hath chosen Zion; he hath desired it for his habitation.

¹⁴ This is my rest for ever: here will I dwell; for I have desired it.

¹⁵ I will abundantly bless her provision: I will satisfy her poor with bread.

¹⁶ I will also clothe her priests with salvation: and her saints shall shout aloud for joy.

¹⁷ There will I make the horn of David to bud: I have ordained a lamp for mine anointed.

¹⁸ His enemies will I clothe with shame: but upon himself shall his crown flourish.

Psalm 133

Behold, how good and how pleasant it is for brethren to dwell together in unity!

2 It is like the precious ointment upon the head, that ran down upon the beard, even Aaron's beard: that went down to the skirts of his garments.

3 As the dew of Hermon, and as the dew that descended upon the mountains of Zion: for there the Lord commanded the blessing, even life for evermore.

Psalm 134

Behold, bless ye the Lord, all ye servants of the Lord, which by night stand in the house of the Lord.

2 Lift up your hands in the sanctuary, and bless the Lord.

3 The Lord that made heaven and earth bless thee out of Zion.

Psalm 135

Praise ye the Lord. Praise ye the name of the Lord; praise him, O ye servants of the Lord.

2 Ye that stand in the house of the Lord, in the courts of the house of our God,

3 Praise the Lord; for the Lord is good: sing praises unto his name; for it is pleasant.

4 For the Lord hath chosen Jacob unto himself, and Israel for his peculiar treasure.

5 For I know that the Lord is great, and that our Lord is above all gods.

6 Whatsoever the Lord pleased, that did he in heaven, and in earth, in the seas, and all deep places.

[7] He causeth the vapours to ascend from the ends of the earth; he maketh lightnings for the rain; he bringeth the wind out of his treasuries.

[8] Who smote the firstborn of Egypt, both of man and beast.

[9] Who sent tokens and wonders into the midst of thee, O Egypt, upon Pharaoh, and upon all his servants.

[10] Who smote great nations, and slew mighty kings;

[11] Sihon king of the Amorites, and Og king of Bashan, and all the kingdoms of Canaan:

[12] And gave their land for an heritage, an heritage unto Israel his people.

[13] Thy name, O Lord, endureth for ever; and thy memorial, O Lord, throughout all generations.

[14] For the Lord will judge his people, and he will repent himself concerning his servants.

[15] The idols of the heathen are silver and gold, the work of men's hands.

[16] They have mouths, but they speak not; eyes have they, but they see not;

[17] They have ears, but they hear not; neither is there any breath in their mouths.

[18] They that make them are like unto them: so is every one that trusteth in them.

[19] Bless the Lord, O house of Israel: bless the Lord, O house of Aaron:

[20] Bless the Lord, O house of Levi: ye that fear the Lord, bless the Lord.

[21] Blessed be the Lord out of Zion, which dwelleth at Jerusalem. Praise ye the Lord.

Psalm 136

O give thanks unto the Lord; for his mercy endureth for ever.

[2] O give thanks unto the God of gods: for his mercy endureth for ever.

[3] O give thanks to the Lord of lords: for his mercy endureth for ever.

[4] To him who alone doeth great wonders: for his mercy endureth for ever.

[5] To him that by wisdom made the heavens: for his mercy endureth for ever.

[6] To him that stretched out the earth above the waters: for his mercy endureth for ever.

[7] To him that made great lights: for his mercy endureth for ever.

[8] The sun to rule by day: for his mercy endureth for ever.

[9] The moon and stars to rule by night: for his mercy endureth for ever.

[10] To him that smote Egypt in their firstborn: for his mercy endureth for ever.

[11] And brought out Israel from among them: for his mercy endureth for ever.

[12] With a strong hand, and with a stretched out arm: for his mercy endureth for ever.

[13] To him which divided the Red sea into parts: for his mercy endureth for ever.

[14] And made Israel to pass through the midst of it: for his mercy endureth for ever,

[15] But overthrew Pharaoh and his host in the Red sea: for his mercy endureth for ever.

¹⁶ To him which led his people through the wilderness: for his mercy endureth for ever.

¹⁷ To him which smote great kings: for his mercy endureth for ever.

¹⁸ And slew famous kings: for his mercy endureth for ever.

¹⁹ Sihon king of the Amorites: for his mercy endureth for ever.

²⁰ And Og the king of Bashan: for his mercy endureth for ever,

²¹ And gave their land for an heritage: for his mercy endureth for ever.

²² Even an heritage unto Israel his servant: for his mercy endureth for ever.

²³ Who remembered us in our low estate: for his mercy endureth for ever.

²⁴ And hath redeemed us from our enemies: for his mercy endureth for ever.

²⁵ Who giveth food to all flesh: for his mercy endureth for ever.

²⁶ O give thanks unto the God of heaven: for his mercy endureth for ever.

Psalm 137

By the rivers of Babylon, there we sat down, yea, we wept, when we remembered Zion.

² We hanged our harps upon the willows in the midst thereof.

³ For there they that carried us away captive required of us a song; and they that wasted us required of us mirth, saying, Sing us one of the songs of Zion.

⁴ How shall we sing the Lord's song in a strange land?

⁵ If I forget thee, O Jerusalem, let my right hand forget her cunning.

[6] If I do not remember thee, let my tongue cleave to the roof of my mouth; if I prefer not Jerusalem above my chief joy.

[7] Remember, O lord, the children of Edom in the day of Jerusalem; who said, Rase it, rase it, even to the foundation thereof.

[8] O daughter of Babylon, who art to be destroyed; happy shall he be, that rewardeth thee as thou hast served us.

[9] Happy shall he be, that taketh and dasheth thy little ones against the stones.

Psalm 138

I will praise thee with my whole heart: before the gods will I sing praise unto thee.

[2] I will worship toward thy holy temple, and praise thy name for thy lovingkindness and for thy truth: for thou hast magnified thy word above all thy name.

[3] In the day when I cried thou answeredst me, and strengthenedst me with strength in my soul.

[4] All the kings of the earth shall praise thee, O Lord, when they hear the words of thy mouth.

[5] Yea, they shall sing in the ways of the Lord: for great is the glory of the Lord.

[6] Though the Lord be high, yet hath he respect unto the lowly: but the proud he knoweth afar off.

[7] Though I walk in the midst of trouble, thou wilt revive me: thou shalt stretch forth thine hand against the wrath of mine enemies, and thy right hand shall save me.

[8] The Lord will perfect that which concerneth me: thy mercy, O Lord, endureth for ever; forsake not the works of thine own hands.

Psalm 139

O Lord, thou hast searched me, and known me.

² Thou knowest my downsitting and mine uprising, thou understandest my thought afar off.

³ Thou compassest my path and my lying down, and art acquainted
with all my ways.

⁴ For there is not a word in my tongue, but, lo, O Lord, thou
knowest it altogether.

⁵ Thou hast beset me behind and before, and laid thine hand upon
me.

⁶ Such knowledge is too wonderful for me; it is high, I cannot attain
unto it.

⁷ Whither shall I go from thy spirit? or whither shall I flee from thy
presence?

⁸ If I ascend up into heaven, thou art there: if I made my bed in
hell, behold, thou art there.

⁹ If I take the wings of the morning, and dwell in the uttermost
parts of the sea;

¹⁰ Even there shall thy hand lead me, and thy right hand shall hold
me.

¹¹ If I say, Surely the darkness shall cover me; even the night shall
be light about me.

¹² Yea, the darkness hideth not from thee; but the night shineth as
the day: the darkness and the light are both alike to thee.

¹³ For thou hast possessed my reins: thou hast covered me in my
mother's womb.

¹⁴ I will praise thee; for I am fearfully and wonderfully made: marvellous are thy works; and that my soul knoweth right well.

¹⁵ My substance was not hid from thee, when I was made in secret,
and curiously wrought in the lowest parts of the earth.

¹⁶ Thine eyes did see my substance, yet being unperfect; and in thy book all my members were written, which in continuance were fashioned, when as yet there was none of them.

¹⁷ How precious also are thy thoughts unto me, O God! how great is the sum of them!

¹⁸ If I should count them, they are more in number than the sand: when I awake, I am still with thee.

¹⁹ Surely thou wilt slay the wicked, O God: depart from me therefore, ye bloody men.

²⁰ For they speak against thee wickedly, and thine enemies take thy name in vain.

²¹ Do not I hate them, O Lord, that hate thee! and am not I grieved with those that rise up aginst thee?

²² I hate them with perfect hatred: I count them mine enemies.

²³ Search me, O God, and know my heart: try me, and know my thoughts:

²⁴ And see if there be any wicked way in me, and lead me in the way everlasting.

Psalm 140

Deliver me, O Lord, from the evil man: preserve me from the violent man;

² Which imagine mischiefs in their heart; continually are they gathered together for war.

³ They have sharpened their tongues like a serpent; adders' poison is under their lips. Selah.

⁴ Keep me, O Lord, from the hands of the wicked; preserve me from the violent man; who have purposed to overthrow my goings.

⁵ The proud have hid a snare for me, and cords; they have spread a net by the wayside; they have set gins for me. Selah.

⁶ I said unto the Lord, thou art my God: hear the voice of my supplications, O Lord.

⁷ O God the Lord, the strength of my salvation, thou hast covered my head in the day of battle.

⁸ Grant not, O Lord, the desires of the wicked: further not his wicked device; lest they exalt themselves. Selah.

⁹ As for the head of those that compass me about, let the mischief of their own lips cover them.

¹⁰ Let burning coals fall upon them: let them be cast into the fire; into deep pits, that they rise not up again.

¹¹ Let not an evil speaker be established in the earth: evil shall hunt the violent man to overthrow him.

¹² I know that the Lord will maintain the cause of the afflicted, and the right of the poor.

¹³ Surely the righteous shall give thanks unto thy name: the upright shall dwell in thy presence.

Psalm 141

Lord, I cry unto thee: make haste unto me: give ear unto my voice, when I cry unto thee.

² Let my prayer be set forth before thee as incense; and the lifting up of my hands as the evening sacrifice.

³ Set a watch, O Lord, before my mouth; keep the door of my lips.

⁴ Incline not my heart to any evil thing, to practice wicked works with men that work iniquity: and let me not eat of their dainties.

⁵ Let the righteous smite me; it shall be a kindness: and let him reprove me; it shall be an excellent oil, which shall not break my head: for yet my prayer also shall be in their calamities.

⁶ When their judges are overthrown in stony places, they shall hear my words; for they are sweet.

⁷ Our bones are scattered at the grave's mouth, as when one cutteth and cleaveth wood upon the earth.

⁸ But mine eyes are unto thee, O God the Lord: in thee is my trust; leave not my soul destitute.

⁹ Keep me from the snares which they have laid for me, and the gins of the workers of iniquity.

¹⁰ Let the wicked fall into their own nets, whilst that I withal escape.

Psalm 142

I cried unto the Lord with my voice; with my voice unto the Lord did I make my supplication.

² I poured out my complaint before him; I shewed before him my trouble.

³ When my spirit was overwhelmed within me, then thou knewest my path. In the way wherein I walked have they privily laid a snare for me.

⁴ I looked on my right hand, and beheld, but there was no man that would know me: refuge failed me; no man cared for my soul.

⁵ I cried unto thee, O Lord: I said, Thou art my refuge and my portion in the land of the living.

⁶ Attend unto my cry; for I am brought very low: deliver me from my persecutors; for they are stronger than I.

⁷ Bring my soul out of prison, that I may praise thy name: the righteous shall compass me about; for thou shalt deal bountifully with me.

Psalm 143

Hear my prayer, O Lord, give ear to my supplications: in thy faithfulness answer me, and in thy righteousness.

² And enter not into iudgment with thy servant: for in thy sight shall no man living be justified.

³ For the enemy hath persecuted my soul; he hath smitten my life down to the ground; he hath made me to dwell in darkness, as those that have been long dead.

⁴ Therefore is my spirit overwhelmed within me; my heart within me is desolate.

⁵ I remember the days of old; I meditate on all thy works; I muse on the work of thy hands.

⁶ I stretch forth my hands unto thee; my soul thirsteth after thee, as a thirsty land. Selah.

⁷ Hear me speedily, O Lord: my spirit faileth: hide not thy face from me, lest I be like unto them that go down into the pit.

⁸ Cause me to hear thy lovingkindness in the morning; for in thee do I trust: cause me to know the way wherein I should walk; for I lift up my soul unto thee.

⁹ Deliver me, O Lord, from mine enemies; I flee unto thee to hide me.

¹⁰ Teach me to do thy will; for thou art my God: thy spirit is good; lead me into the land of uprightness.

¹¹ Quicken me, O Lord, for thy name's sake: for thy righteousness' sake bring my soul out of trouble.

¹² And of thy mercy cut off mine enemies, and destroy all them that afflict my soul: for I am thy servant.

Psalm 144

Blessed be the Lord my strength, which teacheth my hands to war, and my fingers to fight:

² My goodness, and my fortress; my high tower, and my deliverer; my shield, and he in whom I trust; who subdueth my people under me.

³ Lord, what is man, that thou takest knowledge of him! or the son of man, that thou makest account of him!

⁴ Man is like to vanity: his days are as a shadow that passeth away.

⁵ Bow thy heavens, O Lord, and come down: touch the mountains, and they shall smoke.

⁶ Cast forth lightning, and scatter them: shoot out thine arrows, and destroy them.

⁷ Send thine hand from above: rid me, and deliver me out of great waters, from the hand of strange children;

⁸ Whose mouth speaketh vanity, and their right hand is a right hand of falsehood.

⁹ I will sing a new song unto thee, O God: upon a psaltery and an instrument of ten strings will I sing praises unto thee.

¹⁰ It is he that giveth salvation unto kings: who delivereth David his servant from the hurtful sword.

¹¹ Rid me, and deliver me from the hand of strange children, whose mouth speaketh vanity, and their right hand is a right hand of falsehood.

¹² That our sons may be as plants grown up in their youth; that our daughters may be as corner stones, polished after the similitude of a palace;

¹³ That our garners may be full, affording all manner of store: that our sheep may bring forth thousands and ten thousands in our streets:

¹⁴ That our oxen may be strong to labour; that there be no breaking in, nor going out; that there be no complaining in our streets.

¹⁵ Happy is that people, that is in such a case: yea, happy is that people, whose God is the Lord.

Psalm 145

I will extol thee, my God, O king; and I will bless thy name for ever and ever.

2 Every day will I bless thee; and I will praise thy name for ever and ever.

3 Great is the Lord, and greatly to be praised; and his greatness is unsearchable.

4 One generation shall praise thy works to another, and shall declare thy mighty acts.

5 I will speak of the glorious honour of thy majesty, and of thy wondrous works.

6 And men shall speak of the might of thy terrible acts: and I will declare thy greatness.

7 They shall abundantly utter the memory of thy great goodness, and shall sing of thy righteousness.

8 The Lord is gracious, and full of compassion; slow to anger, and of great mercy.

9 The Lord is good to all: and his tender mercies are over all his works.

10 All thy works shall praise thee, O Lord; and thy saints shall bless thee.

11 They shall speak of the glory of thy kingdom, and talk of thy power;

12 To make known to the sons of men his mighty acts, and the glorious majesty of his kingdom.

13 Thy kingdom is an everlasting kingdom, and thy dominion endureth throughout all generations.

14 The Lord upholdeth all that fall, and raiseth up all those that be bowed down.

¹⁵ The eyes of all wait upon thee; and thou givest them their meat in due season.

¹⁶ Thou openest thine hand, and satisfiest the desire of every living thing.

¹⁷ The Lord is righteous in all his ways, and holy in all his works.

¹⁸ The Lord is nigh unto all them that call upon him, to all that call upon him in truth.

¹⁹ He will fulfil the desire of them that fear him: he also will hear their cry, and will save them.

²⁰ The Lord preserveth all them that love him: but all the wicked will he destroy.

²¹ My mouth shall speak the praise of the Lord: and let all flesh bless his holy name for ever and ever.

Psalm 146

Praise ye the Lord. Praise the Lord, O my soul.

² While I live will I praise the Lord: I will sing praises unto my God while I have any being.

³ Put not your trust in princes, nor in the son of man, in whom there is no help.

⁴ His breath goeth forth, he returneth to his earth; in that very day his thoughts perish.

⁵ Happy is he that hath the God of Jacob for his help, whose hope is in the Lord his God:

⁶ Which made heaven, and earth, the sea, and all that therein is: which keepeth truth for ever:

⁷ Which executeth judgment for the oppressed: which giveth food to the hungry. The Lord looseth the prisoners:

[8] The Lord openeth the eyes of the blind: the Lord raiseth them that are bowed down: the Lord loveth the righteous.

[9] The Lord preserveth the strangers; he relieveth the fatherless and widow: but the way of the wicked he turneth upside down.

[10] The Lord shall reign for ever, even thy God, O Zion, unto all generations. Praise ye the Lord.

Psalm 147

Praise ye the Lord: for it is good to sing praises unto our God; for it is pleasant; and praise is comely.

[2] The Lord doth build up Jerusalem: he gathereth together the outcasts of Israel.

[3] He healeth the broken in heart, and bindeth up their wounds.

[4] He telleth the number of the stars; he calleth them all by their names.

[5] Great is our Lord, and of great power: his understanding is infinite.

[6] The Lord lifteth up the meek: he casteth the wicked down to the ground.

[7] Sing unto the Lord with thanksgiving; sing praise upon the harp unto our God:

[8] Who covereth the heaven with clouds, who prepareth rain for the earth, who maketh grass to grow upon the mountains.

[9] He giveth to the beast his food, and to the young ravens which cry.

[10] He delighteth not in the strength of the horse: he taketh not pleasure in the legs of a man.

[11] The Lord taketh pleasure in them that fear him, in those that hope in his mercy.

[12] Praise the Lord, O Jerusalem; praise thy God, O Zion.

¹³ For he hath strengthened the bars of thy gates; he hath blessed thy children within thee.

¹⁴ He maketh peace in thy borders, and filleth thee with the finest of the wheat.

¹⁵ He sendeth forth his commandment upon earth: his word runneth very swiftly.

¹⁶ He giveth snow like wool: he scattereth the hoarfrost like ashes.

¹⁷ He casteth forth his ice like morsels: who can stand before his cold?

¹⁸ He sendeth out his word, and melteth them: he causeth his wind to blow, and the waters flow.

¹⁹ He sheweth his word unto Jacob, his statutes and his judgments unto Israel.

²⁰ He hath not dealt so with any nation: and as for his judgments, they have not known them. Praise ye the Lord.

Psalm 148

Praise ye the Lord. Praise ye the Lord from the heavens: praise him in the heights.

² Praise ye him, all his angels: praise ye him, all his hosts.

³ Praise ye him, sun and moon: praise him, all ye stars of light.

⁴ Praise him, ye heavens of heavens, and ye waters that be above the heavens.

⁵ Let them praise the name of the Lord: for he commanded, and they were created.

⁶ He hath also stablished them for ever and ever: he hath made a decree which shall not pass.

⁷ Praise the Lord from the earth, ye dragons, and all deeps:

⁸ Fire, and hail; snow and vapours; stormy wind fulfilling his word:

⁹ Mountains, and all hills; fruitful trees, and all cedars:

¹⁰ Beasts, and all cattle; creeping things, and flying fowl:

¹¹ Kings of the earth, and all people; princes, and all judges of the earth:

¹² Both young men, and maidens; old men, and children:

¹³ Let them praise the name of the Lord: for his name alone is excellent; his glory is above the earth and heaven.

¹⁴ He also exalteth the horn of his people, the praise of all his saints; even of the children of Israel, a people near unto him. Praise ye the Lord.

Psalm 149

Praise ye the Lord. Sing unto the Lord a new song, and his praise in the congregation of saints.

² Let Israel rejoice in him that made him: let the children of Zion be joyful in their King,

³ Let them praise his name in the dance: let them sing praises unto him with the timbrel and harp.

⁴ For the Lord taketh pleasure in his people: he will beautify the meek with salvation.

⁵ Let the saints be joyful in glory: let them sing aloud upon their beds.

⁶ Let the high praises of God be in their mouth, and a two-edged sword in their hand;

⁷ To execute vengeance upon the heathen, and punishments upon the people;

⁸ To bind their kings with chains, and their nobles with fetters of iron;

⁹ To execute upon them the judgment written: this honour have all his saints. Praise ye the Lord.

Psalm 150

Praise ye the Lord. Praise God in his sanctuary: praise him in the firmament of his power.

² Praise him for his mighty acts: praise him according to his excellent greatness.

³ Praise him with the sound of the trumpet: praise him with the psaltery and harp.

⁴ Praise him with the timbrel and dance: praise him with stringed instruments and organs.

⁵ Praise him upon the loud cymbals: praise him upon the high sounding cymbals.

⁶ Let every thing that hath breath praise the Lord. Praise ye the Lord.